THE
BASTARD
CHILD

Thanks Moes for
helping me change
lives

The
BASTARD
CHILD

A Story of Hope, Resiliency
and Perseverance.

By

Sean P. Hoggs

Named a Prestigious Ten Outstanding Young American in 2007

authorHOUSE®

AuthorHouse™ LLC
1663 Liberty Drive
Bloomington, IN 47403
www.authorhouse.com
Phone: 1-800-839-8640

Published by AuthorHouse 12/06/2013

ISBN: 978-1-4918-3286-8 (sc)
ISBN: 978-1-4918-3285-1 (hc)
ISBN: 978-1-4918-3287-5 (e)

Library of Congress Control Number: 2013920387

"Don't pray for an easy life, pray for the strength to endure a difficult one."

—Bruce Lee

∞

K.M.C

143

Table of Contents

Foreword

"Each day I awake I know I have one more day
to make a difference in someone's life."

—James Mann

I decided to begin this foreword with a quote that Sean P. Hoggs lives by. His story, The Bastard Child: A Story Hope, Resiliency and Perseverance, is one that many, regardless of race, religion, or creed will truly come to appreciate. I first had the pleasure of meeting Sean eight years ago, and I have come to grow, know and understand him. Moreover, I know him to be an extremely humble human being, to which you will find within the pages of his autobiography.

All of the events and experiences detailed are true and have been recorded as he can recall them. Some names, circumstances and identities have been changed in order to protect the privacy of the various individuals involved. Conversations have also been recorded as remembered, but have not been written as directly documented conversations, yet retold stories. I am sure that you will get the feeling and meaning of the true essence of the events as they took place, just like you were "in the moment." You may not have lived these experiences, but you may recognize some similar situations in your own lives and reevaluate them.

When the world counted him out, he defied the odds . . . Statistics suggested that Sean was to follow the trends of the day in the inner city in which he grew up. According to those statistics he should have ended up dead or incarcerated. However, he chose to persevere in life, despite it all. There were many challenges regarding his remarkable life, but through his journey, he endured through the trials and tribulations that greeted him at every turn. In the end, he emerged as a symbol of hope to many and a testament to resiliency. This book is a humble American success story, one that begins as the Bastard Child.

J.W. Piercy, III.
CEO, Omega H. S., LLC

Preface

I am the common man—an African American, but more importantly an American—who lives in a nation riddled with socioeconomic and societal challenges for minorities and those who live at or below the poverty line, where it is all too easy to make excuses in life and to place blame elsewhere for ones failures. A place where gangs, gun violence, death, and drugs have become an everyday part of life for many inner city communities. A place where a seed of hope must be planted. There is no major television network to share my life story, but I'm compelled to share it through these pages. I owe it to those who share a common background and believe in America and her vast opportunities, who dare to seek the American Dream, to show that there is a level of success one can achieve through hard work and perseverance, despite life and its challenges.

Like the athlete that may come from a broken home or community where drugs and violence rule, those that "make it" to the professional level go on to earn vast riches and America embraces them and shares their [success] story through movies and television; I applaud their hard work and hard-earned level of achievement. However, the fact remains that the vast majority of us will never become professional athletes. Moreover, the percentages are against it; therefore, a realistic life story must be brought forth for others to mirror and use as an example outside of the stereotypical example presented in the media today.

My story is a painful American success story, but more importantly, a story of hope. Instead of using the percentage-challenged professional sports vehicle or gangs to rise above the fray, I used the most proven instrument known to man to succeed—an education!

I ask, why then was I chosen to bear such a heavy burden in life? The simple answer is to show that despite overwhelming odds, one can achieve anything in life. Remember, no one said life would be easy. Please read these pages from start to finish. This is my life story . . .

Chapter 1

The Perfect Storm

My mother was born and raised in Easton, Pennsylvania, located in the eastern part of PA. For a black family, Easton was a town of racial equality and was considered affluent for African Americans. My mother, by today's account, grew up in the "Burbs!" One weekend in 1966, my mother had a childhood friend who invited her to spend the weekend in a town called Plainfield located in central New Jersey, about 45 minutes from Easton. Her friend lived on the "West End" of Plainfield. It fast became a custom for my mother to spend her weekends in Plainfield.

During one of those weekend trips, my mother caught the local "59" bus to Elizabeth, NJ. She was going to do some shopping before heading to PA. Upon arriving back to Plainfield via East 5th street, her eye caught this tall handsome "china-black" looking man, as she put it; he was "fine!" From that moment, according to her, she knew she had to meet him. The next time she saw him, he was driving a yellow sports car on Park Avenue and West 5th Street. She continued to come to Plainfield, NJ and finally got to meet him at the Red Tower eatery, which still stands to this day. They began to date each other immediately, and like a turbulent storm at its beginning, it was the birth of the perfect storm.

My mother still worked and lived in Easton, but made it her business to see my father every weekend. She eventually moved to Plainfield two weeks before the riots of 1967 visited New Jersey. By June of 1967, my mother knew she was pregnant with me, conceived at the Rainbow Motel on Route 22 in New Jersey. My father, at the time, worked at National Starch Chemical and promised to provide support to my mother. He still lived with his parents and my mother moved in with the Stevens' on Rock Avenue in Piscataway, NJ and awaited my birth.

During the summer months after the Riot (according to my mother), my father became increasingly jealous. My mother said he became so insanely jealous that he "carried a container or liquid acid" in his car, just for her! Given that fact, you can only imagine what life would be like in the years to come for me. My mother was a strikingly beautiful woman, which fueled the jealousy of my father (according to her). My father swore that he would "disfigure her face" if he ever caught her with another man at the beginning of their relationship. My mom was never scared of my father; deep down, I believe that my father knew that if he harmed my mother she would kill him. At some point, the acid no longer was used as leverage.

During my mother's pregnancy, the time came to give me a name. Well, what should have been a non-event was anything but according to my mother. She had decided to name me Sean after the actor Sean Connery, who she jokingly claimed was the only white man that she ever loved. I was given the middle name Pernell, derived from the Bonanza actor Pernell Roberts, who my mother claimed was the only white man that she would ever marry. However, my father had other plans; he wanted to name me Guy, after him. My mom, a very straightforward person, told my father that the name Guy sounded like a name for a dog, (I actually like the name). Upon making that statement, according to my mother, my father pulled out a handgun and put it to her head with his finger on the trigger. He told her that if she did not name me Guy he would blow her brains out. She stood her ground and told my father "if this is how I am meant to die, then so be it, pull the trigger!" My mother is still alive to this day, so she called his bluff. These are the parents I was born to . . . crazy!

On February 10th, 1968 I was born a child out of wedlock, *a bastard* by definition, with a painful life journey awaiting me. I was small in size, tiny enough that my first crib was a dresser drawer, and a son to a newly married man just twenty-one days after my birth, to his new wife (not my mother) and their daughter, to include another half brother on the other side of town from yet another woman. All three siblings were born within twelve months of one another; papa indeed was "a rolling stone!"

Eventually my mother and father got past their tumultuous storm of a relationship. Although my mother had truly moved on, my father had not. When my mother began to date other men, it became a serious problem for my father, although he was married, a newlywed; as my mother put it, he began to stalk her. According to her, some evenings when she would go home after a night out, as she would be putting her key in her front door, my father would jump out of the bushes on her saying, "At anytime that I want you dead, it's that simple." There were other times when my father would come to see me and refused to leave once he was in the house.

One evening when my father came to visit me, when my mother was going out on a date, she was giving me a quick bath before leaving;

she had planned on taking me to my Godmother's house. My father, also a strong willed person, told my mother's date the he would not be leaving, that he was staying there with his son! My mother looked at her date and my father and stated "I'm leaving," and that's just what she did, not taking me to my godmother's. After returning later that evening from a night out, my mother walked into her home to find my father and me asleep on the couch. Eventually my mother chose to put an end to my father's "in and out" of her life antics.

My father and mother at some point established a tolerant relationship. Eventually they went to court over custody for me and my father was ordered to pay child support and medical care. As a result of the court ruling and after the blood test, along with joint custody, each parent had custody of me for 6 months until I reached the age of 18, which is ironic, because by age 16 I did not have a pot to piss in or a window to throw it out of, let alone medical care! I would not get to know my father in a parental way until years later. However, I am thankful for one thing, that they met, and both decided to donate the sperm and egg that created me (in their perfect storm of a relationship). However volatile the relationship, they gave me life. Without them, I would not be able to share my story. For that reason alone, I'd like to thank my mother and father.

The year was 1973, a challenging time for the country. The Vietnam War was winding down and America was still recovering from the ugly scar that overt racism had created. Plainfield was slowly recovering from the neighboring Newark, NJ riots of the late 1960's that had spilled over into the Queen City. It should have been a time that a child could simply be a child and the only worries of the day would be the streetlights coming on and ending the day. However, for me, it represented a time in my life that haunts me to this day.

Chapter 2

Everything That Glitters Isn't Gold

Mike, as my mother called him, was her live-in boyfriend. A Vietnam Veteran who was the Jekyll and Hyde of my early childhood, and the source of my nightmares at the time. He was from a neighboring town in New Jersey and the man who served as a surrogate father to me; my biological father was not a part of my life at the time despite the court order. Mike worked construction and was a towering man to a six-year-old child. He was good with his hands from what I can remember. His passion for the outdoors sticks out in my mind, and he loved to hunt and fish. Initially I enjoyed having Mike around. He taught me how to ride a bike, fish, and made for some great times; he was for all purposes my dad.

The drive-in movie was a must for Mike as a family. I enjoyed the hotdogs, the ride to the movies, and I loved the Mustang he drove; life was good, or so I thought. Mike would even wake up with me on Saturday mornings and watch cartoons at times. He had no problem with helping me dig into the cereal box to grab that coveted toy or to help me with putting the prize puzzle together that came in the box too. But everything that glitters isn't gold! I know my mind has blocked out quite a bit of this part of my life, but there are some things I simply can't forget. Who Mike was when he first appeared in my life, the warm and caring father-like figure, and who he actually was were in stark contrast of one another!

Camelot soon began to crumble and my nightmare began. The ghosts of the Vietnam War began to plague the home. Slowly, the house was beginning to turn into a house of horrors. Mike's Post Traumatic Stress Disorder demons were beginning to haunt the atmosphere from the war. In fact, he would spend countless hours combing over his photo albums from his combat tour in Vietnam. It was as if Mike was becoming obsessed with them.

At first he would sit me down and just show me the photos in the albums, but it eventually turned into him reliving the war with me. He would make me sit down over and over again with him and then point out every soldier that died during the war. The photos were becoming scary to me because he would go into such graphic detail about each soldiers death. I was six years of age, confused and scared. Mike would repeatedly ask, "Why man, why?" I didn't know what to say or what to do. I sat quietly, praying that I didn't turn into the object of his rage and anger. I knew it was not a matter of if, but when, he would lash out in some way.

Now terrified of the man that I lived with, he began to take his anger and depression out on my mother, the house and me. The nightmare began early for me. I was riding my bike with the other kids in the neighborhood and as kids do, we became creative with our little bikes, meaning we made ramps and used our bikes to jump over them (very small ramps made with scrap wood, maybe a foot off of the ground). Ultimately I ended up breaking the chain on my bike and I had to walk it home; a bike that Mike had purchased with his hard earned money and taught me how to ride.

When I got home, I did not think too much of it. I told my mother that I had popped the chain on my bike and she told me to put the bike on the side of the house and that Mike would fix it when he got home from work. So I did as she told me and then came into the house, washed up, and got ready for dinner. Shortly thereafter Mike came home from work, tired and hungry as I can imagine (empathetically as a man now).

At the dinner table, my mother said "Mike, Sean broke the chain on his bike. Could you take a look at it and see if you can fix it?" He paused, and asked me "What happened?" I explained to him that we were jumping our bikes on the ramp that we had made and that I had broken my chain by [accident]. I sat there not knowing what to expect, the atmosphere and moment was tense. Mike then gently placed his fork down. My little heart was pounding with fear, and suddenly the reality of the moment manifested its self upon me, the discipline would be instantaneous. The bike was gone the next day but not the haunting memory of the night. It would take days before I was in any position to go outside from the events of that evening. I'm not sure what my mother did to address it afterwards (the severity of the discipline); but, I do know whatever she did or said didn't work. The horror continued for me and I felt like a prisoner in my own home.

The Mayer's lived around the corner from us. They treated me like a true family member and were very kind to me from what I can recall. When Mike began to impose his will on the home, my mom would send me over there, sometimes for nights on end, until whatever demons Mike was dealing with had subsided. I knew at the Mayer's home there was love and they functioned as a tight knit nuclear unit. Of the time with Mike, going to the Mayer's home became one of two escapes that I could get away to. The second was Gerri (Danielle to many), my friend who lived on the corner. Gerri was always there for me, as I believe that most people in the neighborhood understood that something was going on in my home. Although we were just little kids, she was like the sister I never had. To escape Mike, I would wake up early in the morning to go and play with her.

Unlike today, kids were allowed to roam their neighborhood knowing that the parents were there to watch over all of the children. I knew I could knock on Gerri's door early in the morning and her parents would let me in. Gerri would always come to the door with a big smile and give me a huge hug, at times wiping the sleep out of her eyes with her pajamas on. She would tell me "I'll be right back," and then she would go and get dressed while I anxiously awaited her return. On the weekends, at times, we would sit in her living room and watch cartoons all morning before she got dressed. We sat right next to each other and Gerri gave me such a sense of comfort, even sharing cereal bowls at times.

Although she suffered from asthma badly, she always made sure that I was okay. Breakfast at her house was breakfast for me as well, if I hadn't eaten at home. Sometimes I really didn't care if I ate breakfast at home; I just wanted to get out of there before [he] woke up. I no longer looked forward to sharing Saturday mornings with Mike; he was not the same man, and the friendly mask that he wore in the beginning when I first met him was now his true face, that of a monster. I told Gerri that I was scared of the man in my house and made her promise not to tell anyone. She would always hug me then kiss me on the cheek and say that she would protect me.

When it was time for me to go home, she knew I was terrified; she would walk me to my door and say "I'll see you tomorrow." Gerri knew what I was in for. I could see her house from mine and she would always stand on the curb in front of her house to wave bye once she made it back home. That would remain our routine until I was sent away. To this day, we still remain very close; few, if any, know of our relationship. I've since thanked her for being there for me. We jokingly call each other sandbox buddies now because back then, she had a sandbox in her back yard and we would spend countless hours in that sandbox. It was our universe and no one else mattered. The world came to a standstill when we were together. If people only understood the level of safety and comfort she gave me. Gerri, I love you for that and thank you!

When night would fall, I never knew what type of evening would transpire. I would eat dinner, trying not to look at Mike because I didn't want a repeat of the bike incident. I was traumatized to say the least. I tried my best not to set him off. If there were races for speed eating back then for six-year-olds, hands down I would have won a gold medal! I feared the dinner table, the one place where American families came together to be a family! All I knew was the sooner I got through eating dinner, the sooner I got away from him.

After dinner, most nights I would make my way upstairs to take a bath. I had a bag full of toys and I would make it by business to stay in the tub as long as I could in order to avoid Mike. I would always lock the door, terrified that he was going to come in and try to drown me, which in reality I knew my mother would not allow. The sound of the stairs creaking when Mike walked up them made my little heart pound. Routinely he would stop by the bathroom door and stand right outside of it for no other reason than to mess with my psyche; well, it worked! I would watch the doorknob, my eyes glued to it like a hawk, praying that he didn't try to enter (which he never did).

Once I would actually get in the bed, most nights I would fall asleep with the television on in my room (strangely, it gave me a sense of comfort). It was at that point that my mom had to deal with another aspect of terror with Mike. My mom would frantically come into my room and tell me to lock the door. At age six, not knowing why, I did. I would ball up by the door at times and listen while my mom dealt with Mike! I would hear them yelling and screaming at one another, not sure of what was going on. At six, I would try my best to help my mother, but she would always rush me back into my room. I was young, my father nowhere to be found (I really didn't know of him); what could I do? I tried! Those nights sadly became the norm and I wanted so badly for him to just go away—Mars, Pluto, anywhere far away! It even got to the point that my mother would wake me out of my sleep and take me to Patricia's house (Matriarch of the Mayer family) before he got started. Sometimes I would return home from the Mayer's to see dishes broken on the floor and walls, end tables smashed, food all over the place, and the house completely in utter shambles.

Mentally, everything began to take its toll on me! I began secretly sleeping on the floor by the door of my room for weeks on end regardless if I heard something or not, hoping that it would stop Mike from getting to me (even with the door locked). No one was spared from his demons. I was terrified of the night. For those moments when Mike and I were alone in his car, he would repeatedly torment me over and over again. I'm not sure if he resented the fact that I was not his son or if he was just a lost soul. Again, the tormenting would go on until I was sent away. I believed sooner or later he would try to kill us! His anger was unimaginable. Before long, Mike and his Vietnam friends were fixtures in the house. Drugs, war stories, and the daily struggles with Mike (regarding me and my mother) and his demons were all too familiar to me by then. I just couldn't handle it anymore!

One day when my mother picked me up from the babysitters, I refused to go home. I fought my mother with all I had, even breaking my lunch box over her out of fear. To say she was enraged is an understatement. When she finally got me home, after a fierce struggle on my part, I raced up the stairs hoping to beat her to the bathroom where I could lock the bathroom door, my sanctuary. Well, it was not to be, my mother raced up the stairs right behind me and forced her way into the bathroom when I tried to close the door. The force that she opened the bathroom door with drove the metal doorknob straight into my nose. I was knocked unconscious immediately!

When I regained consciousness, I was on the bathroom floor with blood all around me, (on the floor, my shirt and pants); my mother had me in her arms and she was trying to clean up all of the blood. I couldn't believe what had just happened; I felt alone at that point, dejected! It would take weeks for my nose to heal and I never went to the hospital. I found myself in the house for an extended period again, this time with a swollen face and two blackened eyes.

Yes, mentally I was spent! I was tired of sleeping on the floor by the door at night when my mother left my room out of fear, getting tormented by Mike, hearing my mother deal with the madness and locking my bedroom door in a place that I should feel safe, no more! At that point, my mother knew changes had to be made because I was beginning to shut down. She had also hurt the child that she had tried to protect all this time. Mike, I believe, may have also told my mother at some point that he was going to kill us all, and she believed him.

Abruptly, I was packed up and sent to live with my mother's first husband and family, in Altamonte Springs, FL, a man and family I knew absolutely nothing about. I didn't know that my mother had been previously married and I was never told that I had a brother. However, now aware of my mother's previous marriage, I thought that things would be better for me there, but I was mistaken—horribly mistaken! I didn't get a chance to say goodbye to Gerri, the Mayer's, or even Mike's parents or siblings, who were very good to me, ironically. All things taken into account, it was as if my mother knew that Mike, an infantry combat veteran of the Vietnam War, and a man that could and had killed, was going to follow through on his words.

Chapter 3

The Sunshine State

I remember the flight to Florida; I was alone. My mother had walked me to the departing gate. I remember being walked down the tunnel that led to the aircraft by the stewardess and being placed in my seat. Confused, I wondered where my mother was. From what I can recall, she never told me that she was not coming too. Too young to understand the gravity of the entire situation, all I could do is cry, and that I did! I remember thinking that wherever I was going, my mother would be there to get me, but I was wrong! The stewardess had given me a small plastic airplane to play with and it served as little comfort to me at that time.

While the rest of the passengers got on the aircraft, I was hoping and praying that my mother was going to be one of them, but eventually the plane was boarded by all the passengers and we taxied down the runway. My mother was nowhere to be found and the plane took flight; I was alone and scared. Not scared of the flight, scared of the unknown! Once I arrived in Florida (it could have been Mars for all that mattered), the stewardess walked me off of the airplane. The Captain of the flight handed me another plastic airplane as I departed, I guess to say good job for not going crazy mid-flight.

When I walked off of the aircraft, I was desperately looking for my mother. My little mind refused to accept that she was still in New Jersey. The woman waiting for me was not my mother; it was Amelia, my mother's mother-in law. She was a massive woman to me, a lot bigger than my mother. She had a single gold cap on her tooth that stood out when she smiled; it was the first thing I noticed. She gave me a big hug and said that she was my Grandmother. She was my Grandmother by marriage but not by blood. Once we got my luggage, off we went to her home, my new home.

Upon pulling up to the house, the first thing I noticed was that the neighborhood seemed totally different from mine. It was dark, and unlike in New Jersey, there were no streetlights. The sounds of the south were deafening. I heard frogs croaking, dogs barking far and near, and things jumping around in the grass as we approached the house. For all it's worth, I was a city kid! Young yes, but I knew nothing about the South and the sounds of the night that came with it. Once I entered the house, there were a lot of people there to greet me. Everyone seemed so nice; I thought that this might be okay while I tried to take it all in, yet my mind wondered where my mother was.

As the family started to introduce themselves, they could have been the Jetsons for all the mattered. Big Jeff, my half-brother's father, was there and greeted me as well. He gave me a sense of comfort strangely, but nothing removed my want for my mother, my security blanket. I met my stepbrothers by marriage, Kyle and Tony, as well as Bret, Amelia's son. I remember that Kyle had my plastic airplanes after I sat them down and I wanted them back. Terrified to say anything to the strangers that I had just met, I kept my little mouth shut and said nothing.

While getting settled into the home in the weeks to follow, I found myself asking Amelia daily, if not religiously, where was my mother and could I call her on the phone? At first Amelia was very accommodating, she would tell me that my mother was fine or that I had just missed her call. I wanted my mother to know that I loved her and that I wanted to come home, yes, even if I had to endure the madness. I never did get to speak to her initially and it would be months before I would actually talk to her on the phone. Feeling a profound sense of guilt, I blamed myself for the situation that was at hand. I was devastated and I really felt that my mother didn't want me anymore; what else was I to think?

Strikingly, I looked just like my mother, even at a young age. Whatever drove my mother and Jeff apart (from my vantage point) enraged Amelia and I could begin to see the hate that she had for my mother, who they called "Mona," begin to manifest itself on me. She would always say, "You look" or, "You act just like your Mother." She was my mom, so on that note, I guess Amelia was right. My question, why send me to Florida? That warm and inviting smile that had greeted me at the airport was no more.

Amelia was not the one to spare the rod to spoil the child, especially with me! Unlike my mother, the church was a staple for Amelia. We spent what seemed like every day at the church, me Kyle, Brent, Tony, and Jeff. Although Kyle and Tony's mom was still around, I did not have my mother. The ritual was chores, school, homework, and church, everyday. Not that I did not like God, but for a kid at my age, I wanted to go outside and play sometimes; Amelia would have nothing of the sort, at least for me. As the time passed, I just came to the realization that my mother was gone; I hadn't heard from her in so long that I remember forgetting what her voice sounded like.

Oddly one day, Amelia called me into her room. She said, "Sean, I want you to call me mom!" I said, "But you are not my mother." She then slapped me across the face and said, "You will call me mom!" It was at that point that things really began to get bad for me. However I ended up in Florida, whether it was because of Mike, or for some reason still unbeknownst to me today, Amelia never intended to give me back.

Although I was just a child, I knew one thing, Amelia was not my mother and I was not going to call her mom! I even hated calling her Grandmom; the Grandmother I knew lived in Easton, Pennsylvania and she was good to me. Amelia was anything but. I felt like Cinderella with no hopes of having a fairy Godmother, or slipping my foot into a glass slipper. I was the little Bastard Child trapped in another situation with my hands tied.

In Amelia's eyes, I was a demon seed. I was constantly told again and again that I was just like my mother. Add to that, each time I would call Amelia Grandmom, I would literally get slapped. My brother Jeff would tell me to just go along with it, but I refused! Each time I refused, it would reinforce the disdain Amelia had for my mother, and her anger would manifest in other ways for me. I fast became the one who had the lion's share of the chores in the house.

Big Jeff was my only source of relief. He did not live in the house but he came by daily. He treated me as if I was his own son. I actually began to look forward to him stopping by. Jeff would take us to get hamburgers and fries from a local restaurant from time-to-time, which for a kid was heaven. An occasional trip to the movies and Sea World with Jeff let me escape the mental and physical abuse I was enduring at Amelia's hands. I did not tell him what was going on for fear of reprisal. I just couldn't understand why I was always the object of someone else's rage, hate or anger; I was just a child! Looking back, I realize that I was just a pawn in a greater game with my mother. However, that game proved to be emotionally painful and very physically abusive for me.

Now with the holidays in season, Amelia, who did not make a lot of money, was naturally frugal. I received the hand-me-downs from my brother Jeff who was four years older than me. I was a small child, and Jeff was husky. So to wear his used clothes I looked like something right out of a three-ring circus, not to mention how bad I was ridiculed at school. Jeff, by way of his father, always had nice clothes. Kyle and Tony, by way of Big Jeff and their mother, had nice clothes. But it simply was not the case for me. My one hope in getting something new was during Christmas. I just knew that I would finally get something that was not handed down, but I was wrong.

My one Christmas while living in Florida, I remember my brother Jeff, Bret, Kyle, and Tony all had plenty of gifts to go around. I just knew that my mother had sent money down to get me some gifts for Christmas. I anxiously waited to open my gifts, but I waited for everyone else to open theirs. I did not want to upset Amelia. Finally, I was handed one gift. Thinking there were more, I remember looking at Amelia as to say where are my other gifts like everyone else? But there were no other gifts. When I opened the box, it was one pair of pants. I was thankful for what I had received, but I was hurt. Hurt because I really knew that I was an outsider. Amelia made it clear to everyone that day that I was not a relative by blood, but by marriage. I remember thinking that everyone hated me. I went into the back room to be by myself as Jeff, Bret, Kyle, and Tony enjoyed a hearty Christmas.

Big Jeff, seeing what had just been done to me in front of everyone, would make amends and buy me a few more things in the days to come; he was truly a good man. But the damage was done mentally for me. My brother offered up to share his toys with me. Kyle and Tony's toys went home with them to Gayle's. Looking back it was an evil and nasty thing to do to a child, to make a point at a time of forgiveness and understanding, especially for a "woman of the church!"

The games that Amelia played would escalate. She began to speak to me like a dog—nasty, always in a demeaning tone. To me, what appeared to be one of her favorite sayings was, "Sean I'm going to beat you." It echoes in my soul to this day. If something was not done to her standard, a double standard for me, then a beating was guaranteed. "Switch's" were readily available in the back yard and I had grown accustomed to getting one. Nothing was ever done right by me or met her standards, so I just became numb to the beatings. If the beds weren't made, hers in particular, it was a beating! If the dishes weren't done, it was a beating! If the trash was not taken out, it was a beating! It got to the point that my brother would go behind me just to make sure that everything was done right, but it did not matter. No one else in that house was dealing with the beatings but me.

Amelia hated my mother, and she was taking it out on me. The sheer force by which she would beat me, by today's standards would surely have had her locked up. But who could I turn to? Who could I tell? I felt trapped. My brother could not say anything or he would catch it. If I said something at school, they would call home asking the necessary questions and I would get it! I really did not know what to do. Amelia was a charmer, and who was I to disclose a monster to everyone? I was a child, the Bastard Child, and an outsider.

When I finally got to talk to my mother on the phone, I told her everything that was going on. It was as if she wasn't hearing me. Whatever situation drove me down south still had a grip on her (Mike, finances, drugs, who knows); she would just say that everything would be all right. In my mind I was saying, "Lady, get me out of here . . . This woman is crazy!" However, my mother was calling for a particular reason this time. Mike had killed himself. She was calling to let me know. To be honest, I felt a sense of relief because I was really terrified of him. Maybe Mike was going to kill us all and my mother was right by sending me south. But that was really the extent of the phone call. I'm just thankful that Mike didn't kill my mother.

When I hung up the phone, I had an empty feeling in my stomach. My mother said nothing about getting me out of Florida, although I told her everything that was going on. It's as if she did not want to believe me. But, because of what Mike had just put me through, she knew that I knew what I was talking about. I guess she said, "Sean you'll have to live with the lesser of two evils." Well thanks Mom, that's a lot for a child to swallow! I thought, at least sit me down and say, "Sean, I am sending you to live in Florida and here's why." My question, where was my father since he wanted me so bad and he had joint custody? My theory was that my mother not only sent me away because of Mike and his Post Traumatic Stress Disorder, but to hide me from my father! It's apparent to me now that the two were still playing a nasty custody game with me.

Getting back to Amelia, she knew that I was at her mercy. "Big Ma'am" (Amelia's mother) rarely said anything to me. She was an old school southern woman that said few words. Every Sunday after church we would go over to her house for dinner. Fish and grits and all the traditional southern foods were commonplace at her home. I remember being scared of her because she was bigger than Amelia and Amelia appeared to be very mindful, even fearful, of her. We (the boys) would have to do chores at Big Ma'am's house. I was always told to make the bed in her room and to clean it up. That included dusting, sweeping the floors, and cleaning a spittoon.

I was fine with doing whatever chores that were placed before me; God knows I did not want to set Amelia off, but I really hated cleaning that spittoon, which was a coffee can in all reality. I even asked Amelia if I could clean something else besides that, but of course the answer was always, no! I would actually throw up every time I would clean it. Big Ma'am wanted it dumped and washed out every time I cleaned her room. To look at it, it looked like throw up to me. Amelia knew I hated it and it became another tool by which she could take aim at me. I did not want to stick my hand in the can knowing that spit was in it. I would first dump the can out, and then rinse it with hot water (which was brown and smelled to me), then I had to get the pieces of the tobacco stuck to the can out by hand, my hand! I had to show Amelia the can when I was done and it had to meet her approval. If it did not meet her standard it resulted into another beating, which to me was commonplace by then.

I had to figure out a way to get out of this chore. I knew my solution would result in a painful outcome, but I had to stand my ground just like I did on calling Amelia mom. My plan was simple—dump the spittoon on Big Ma'am's bed. It was one of the many battles between her and me, but she knew I had resolve. Eventually the time came when I was to put my plan into action. It took me a few weeks to muster up the nerve. But as I waited to move, I still had to clean that can. And as I cleaned it, and waited, it gave me the resolve to execute my plan, knowing that I was in for a terrible beating by Amelia's hand as a result. In my head, I kept asking myself, "Why isn't someone else cleaning this thing too?" The simple and short answer was that Amelia knew that this was getting under my skin and that it bothered me. I really hated that spittoon!

The day came and I knew what I was in for. Just like any other Sunday, we went to Big Ma'am's house, and again it was chore time. As stated, I had to clean her room and that disgusting spittoon. But today would be different; today would be the first day that I said no more! As

I cleaned the room, the time had come for the can. It was filled with plenty of chew and spit. I paused and grabbed the can; I took a deep breath knowing what was to follow, and dumped it all over the bed. Big Ma'am had white covers, the old quilted style. I made a beautiful mess of things. I made sure to get the nasty and used chewing tobacco all over the place. It was a defiant moment for me; I had to fight back. None of the other grandchildren had to do this disgusting chore, and I was being told to do it because I was an outsider, a relative by marriage and not by blood, "the Bastard Child!"

When she came in to inspect immediately she noticed the stain. She asked, "What happened?" Nervous and scared I said, "I spilled it on the bed." She said, "By accident?" The look she gave me raced through my bones! I knew what was coming next (before I could even answer) and she would not disappoint, I was beaten about the back and legs!

She seemed to take her anger out on me regarding my mom every time she beat me, I could see the hate in her eyes. But this day, I lashed out and lashed out not just at her, but her mother, the matriarch too. It was a painful stance, but one that had to be taken. I hated crying because I knew she reveled in it! No one else was living this nightmare but me, so no one else was going to fix it but me, in my own way. My mother was worlds away and the one time we did speak, I fell on deaf ears.

The next week came, Amelia believing that she had broken my spirit and that I had learned my lesson, sent me back to Big Ma'am's room for my weekly routine after Sunday dinner. She felt assured that I would not act out again; after all, the scars (although covered, and told if I said anything "I would get some more" of the same) still hurt to the touch. It had only been a week . . . I thought different!

Defiantly again, I meticulously cleaned up Big Ma'am's room, I made the bed up, and swept the floor. I then grabbed the spittoon and poured the disgusting spit and chew all over the bed again! When I was done, Amelia said that she would be in to check, confident that everything was going to be all right. She walked into the room to find Big Ma'am's bed and covers once again filled with the residue of the spittoon. She slapped me to the floor and beat me with her bare hands; but this time I refused to cry and waited for the beating to stop. She told me that I was the "child of the devil;" I was thinking, no I'm an abused child who wants his mother and I'm living with Satan the Bible thumper herself. I never did have to clean Big Ma'am's room or that spittoon again after that. Pouring out that spittoon and cleaning the can with my hands was not in the cards for me one way or another. I wouldn't have anyone do that, let alone a child.

After the spittoon incident, I soon realized that I had won the battle but not the war. Amelia would find other ways to enact her wrath on me. I would not be allowed to go outside for weeks on end. School, chores, no T.V., and off to my room (the back of the house) was my daily ritual. I would watch the other kids play in the neighborhood from the window, to include my brother and stepbrothers (again by marriage, my mother had not legally divorced Big Jeff). It seemed like no matter what I did it just was not good enough. It got to be the case where I was fine being alone by myself (thus why I am somewhat of a loner to this day).

In the morning before school, I would have to go out and start Amelia's school bus (yes, as a child); she drove the bus for the township that we lived in. No big deal, but no one else in the house had to get up early and start that monstrosity of a bus! Bret, her son, was a member of the band and he was her pride and joy. I made it my business to stay as far away from him as possible; he was very weird to me. Of all the members that stayed in that house, I was clearly the outsider. The beatings continued but I refused to cry anymore. Amelia would send me to bed without dinner quite often. My brother Jeff would sneak me food all the time. I looked forward to lunch at Altamonte Elementary. It almost got to be the case where I felt like I was only eating at school.

As the saying goes, "children and drunks do not lie." One day I went to school and I was very hungry. I told my teacher that I hadn't eaten dinner at home the night before and that I was very hungry. My teacher asked me why I had not eaten and I told the truth that I was sent to bed without dinner the night before. She asked me how often did this happen? And me being a kid (not a drunk), I gave her an honest answer. I said all the time. My teacher took me out of class immediately and sent me down to the office where they gave me some crackers and juice.

I ate the crackers and drank my juice thinking I did nothing wrong; I was hungry. When I was done I was sent back to my classroom and I thought nothing more or it. What I did not know, and rightfully so, is that the school was contacting Amelia and asking her about my welfare. I'm not sure what the nature of the discussion was, but Amelia was on her way to the school. Not knowing what was going on, I was sent back to the office. Once Amelia arrived at the school, the school told me to tell Amelia what I had told them. I said "I was hungry because I did not eat dinner last night and that I was sent to bed without dinner." The school sent me back to class. In my mind I had did nothing wrong because I really had been sent to bed without dinner and I really was hungry.

Well, the truth did not "set me free;" it incurred the wrath of Amelia when I got home. She was embarrassed and I was beat unmercifully, yet my little mind could not comprehend what was happening to me because I felt I hadn't done anything wrong. Amelia's message to me was simple; what she did and was doing to me in her house was not to go any further than her and that house! No matter what I said or who I told Amelia did no wrong in anyone's eyes, except for the school that one time. I would tell my mother years later of the abuse I endured while living in that house, because she refused to hear me when I was a child actually going through it the first time. My mother's words to me were, "forgive her and move on!" I told her I can forgive, but I cannot forget, it was a brutal experience! I had endured Mike's Post Traumatic Stress Disorder and tormenting to have to turn around and deal with Amelia and her physical and mental abuse, a lot for a child at 6 and 7 years of age to deal with.

The last thing I recall is being hit in the face with a rock by accident in Florida. I was at the wrong place at the wrong time and I was hit by a rock. The creek by Big Ma'am's house was where the kids would skip rocks. As I was in the creek collecting tadpoles, I was hit in the face by a rock on accident. The kid that hit me immediately came up to me and apologized. The "cat tails" in the creek were high, I can understand how it could have happen. That was not the issue; my eye was badly injured, split to the bone, blood was all over the place [once again], and I made my way to the house. Thinking that I would receive some type of care from Amelia, I instead was greeted by her anger. She asked, "What happened, what did you do!" I told her that I was hit in the face by a rock on accident but she thought I had done something to provoke it, but it just was not the case.

Amelia gave me a washcloth and told me to clean up the blood. Knowing what I know now, I needed stitches, bad, the gash was wide like a boxer's injury! Once again my eye was closed from a blow to it. While it healed, the gnats were always around it I remember. The scar I have on my left eyebrow is a stark reminder of that painful day. The scar has since become a part of my personality. Looking back, it was a cruel thing to do to a child. Had it been Bret, Jeff, Kyle or Tony, without question Amelia would have taken them to the hospital immediately. But no, it was me the little Bastard Child once again left to deal with the hardships of life. Her hate for me was and is simply indescribable.

Eventually my mother found her way to Florida to visit. I eagerly awaited her arrival. Amelia's message to me, I better not say a word about what was happening to me. For me it really did not matter because I had tried to tell my mother before, but she just ignored it! Why? Who knows, but I had the scars to prove it. When she arrived I could barely contain myself; I was in desperate need of my mother's love and touch, but something was wrong; my mother was distant. She carried herself in a manner that I did not recognize. She also appeared to be under the spell of Amelia too. It was as if she wanted to be on her best behavior around her. But why send me there?

We spent a little time together but not much. I was always kept at a distance and I was sent to my room (the back of the house) often while she was there, and my mother allowed it. I think she feared Amelia or craved her acceptance, but whatever it was she had a spell on my mother. When I was finally alone with my mother, I poured my heart out telling her everything that was going on. I did not care if Amelia found out. I just wanted out of that house, bad! My mother would remain in Florida for a week or so, and then she was gone. I just knew that my mother was taking me with her after I told her everything that was going on. After all, my mother said that she would fix it all after we talked.

My brother Jeff actually got to spend the Lion's share of time with my mother. In fact, my mother never told me when she was leaving Florida. I woke up one morning and she was gone. My heart was broken and I felt like I had no one else in the world to turn to. My brother Jeff was there but he was limited in what he could do to protect me. Jeff's father was there for me too, but ultimately I was not his blood child. I was stuck, and God knows I wanted out of there. I would remain there for some time after my mother left and Amelia continued to torment me relentlessly. She began to tell me that my mother did not want me and that's why she left me there. Sadly, I began to believe it!

Chapter 4

There's No Place Like Home

The day finally arrived when my mother called and we spoke; she said, "Sean, I'm bringing you back to New Jersey." I was so happy; I was finally going home. I knew I was finally getting away from Amelia, but I couldn't show my joy outwardly. In fact, my mother only sent for me, and my brother Jeff, a Hoggs by blood, remained in Florida. He didn't have to endure what I did living in that house, so he was fine. I really didn't have any friends to say goodbye to, just Johnny who lived across the street, and I really didn't play with him too much because it seemed like I was always on punishment.

I was ready to go! Big Jeff took me to the Greyhound bus terminal and my brother Jeff was with me. I really was leaving, finally! Maybe my mother heard my cries or my brother Jeff told her that she needed to get me out of there because of Amelia's abuse, but regardless I was leaving, alone on the bus. There was no goodbye from Amelia at all, just painful memories . . .

The bus trip, two days long, seemed like five minutes. I remember arriving to New Jersey and seeing the "Welcome to New Jersey" sign and taking a deep breath and saying to myself, *ah, I'm home, there's no place like it.* At that moment, I had done something that I had not done in a very long time, I simply smiled as a kid! When I arrived, my Aunt Evon and then Uncle Bill (now divorced) actually picked me up from the bus station. I went to stay the night with them before my mother came to pick me up from their house. What was one more night to me? I was safe now . . .

Franklin Place, Plainfield, NJ was home for me now and I was glad to be there. After Mike killed himself, I guess my mother got it together and eventually found an apartment. I did not have a bedroom, but I slept on the couch, which was just fine with me. I was not sleeping under a bed in fear, nor was I sent to a room that felt like a jail cell. I was in a place for the first time in my life that made me happy. I was a kid finally allowed to be a kid.

My mother appeared to be happy, she had a smile to sport and I could see that her soul was at peace. Whatever happened while I was gone, she had cleaned up that mess and she was ready to press on with our life. I really think she heard my cries regarding Florida but her hands were tied by a situation that she had no control over (at least that's what I was telling myself).

Again, I think she had to choose the lesser of two evils for me, and chose the latter; although I think her intentions were well sending me to Florida because of the threats from Mike. She had no idea that Amelia would be so cruel to me. And no, my father still had not become a part of my life, nor did I know or remember what he looked like, but at that point I really didn't care. Things were good and we were living just fine.

The next year or so living on Franklin Place made for great times. Amos was the superintendent who took care of the apartments where we lived. Minnie was his wife and she was like a second mother to all the children in the complex and neighborhood. I quickly made friends, and for the first time in a long while, I felt wanted. My partner in crime fast became Chucky, who lived in the same building. Nicole lived across the court and she was a regular who hung out with Chucky and me.

There were the Spanish sisters, Janelle and Colleen, who lived across the street from the apartment complex. Their house was where all the kids seemed to gravitate to; it could of also have been the fact that their mom loved to cook and there was nothing like their mom's cooking; I love Spanish food and I swear it's because of Janelle and Colleen's mom's cooking way back then. Sherri rounded out the crew and she was the oldest of us all. Our crew was tight and collectively we were having the times of our lives.

In the summer, Amos would ensure we had a source of entertainment; he would hook up the water sprinkler system in the back of the parking lot that served as our water fun. We would all play under that sprinkler for hours making up all kinds of games. Teeth chattering and being chilled to the bone after a full day of play in that sprinkler was pure bliss for us. I was finally able to take part in fun that had been missing for me in Florida.

Colleen, Janelle's little sister, was my first little girlfriend. She was beautiful and her hair smelled so good I remember. We would write each other little love notes and pass them back and forth. She even gave me a picture of her that I kept in my back pocket always. Although just kids, I liked her a lot.

Chucky was my right-hand man. We were mischievous together, always plotting on how we were going to get the latest toys from our parents. I spent just as much time at Chuck's house as I did my own.

His room was on the bottom floor and all I had to do was tap on his window for him to come and open his front door. He had an electric racetrack and we would play with that track for hours on end. If I was not at his apartment, he was at mine. It was almost like living in two different homes at the same time. Yes, life was finally good . . .

Minnie, Amos's wife, was my babysitter while my mother was at work. She was a southern woman but not like Amelia at all. She was kind and considerate. She always had a smile on her face and I do not believe that I ever saw her get mad. She would help me with my homework and she too gave me a great sense of comfort. My guard was always up, given the violent and turbulent events of my past at such a young age. But Minnie remained consistent throughout my time on Franklin Place.

Sherri and Janelle, the two oldest of the crew, were tight. They served as big sisters to us all. Sherri was a beautiful young girl and so was Janelle, Colleen's sister. Between the two of them, they ran the crew. What they said went, and that was it. They would even plan out which ice cream we would buy so that everyone could get a taste of something different. We never fought amongst each other and at the end of the night, we would all agree to meet up at particular time the next day, depending on if school was in recess for Summer or not. Yes, those were the days.

At night I still found it very difficult to sleep. The nightmares and trauma from the past kept haunting me. Although Mike was now deceased, somehow in my little brain, I kept thinking that he was going to hurt me. I would break out into night terrors, screaming at the top of my lungs. My mom would race into the living room where I was asleep and wake me up and say Mike was gone in a comforting and reassuring tone. I even suffered from night terrors while in Florida and my brother Jeff would come to my side. He didn't want Amelia to come into the room where we slept because he knew she would beat me—yes, for having a nightmare. I am in my forties now and I still wake up in a cold sweat, traumatized by the events of my childhood (my children and wife have to wake me up from a distance). During my time living on Franklin Place I did know one thing, I was safe. My subconscious, however, stood guard over me, and certain memories were deeply rooted in my soul. It was trying to protect me.

One day, a man came to visit us at Franklin Place. My mother initially did not tell me who he was; up until that time, my mother hadn't allowed any man into our apartment or lives, I guess because of the ordeal we both lived with Mike. But something was different about this man. He took an interest in me and not my mother. My mother went back into the bedroom as me and this gentleman sat in the living room, my pseudo bedroom; he asked me all kinds of questions, like did I like sports? What was my favorite thing to do? He asked me to stand up, saying he wanted to get a good look at me. He smiled and said you are a skinny little thing aren't you? I shrugged my shoulders as to agree with him. He started to tell me about himself but he never disclosed fully who he was. He told me he had a motorcycle and asked me if I wanted to come outside and see it? I was kid, so I said yes.

We went outside; I cannot recall the make and model of the motorcycle but it was pretty. He asked me if I wanted to sit on it and I said yes. I climbed on the motorcycle, put on the helmet, and grabbed the handlebars. For a brief second, I really enjoyed sitting on that bike. However, after a minute or two, I got off of the bike and gave him his helmet back. He looked at me strangely and said, "What's wrong?" I said "I wanted to go back into the apartment with my mom." Although he was puzzled, I knew exactly what I was doing. I was protecting myself. I was not going to fall for another Mike. I was guarded, and I had become protective of my person.

The man sensing my reluctance said, "let's take a ride on the motorcycle." I just couldn't resist, so I said "okay." He told me to grab around his waist and to hold on tight. Off we went into the streets of Plainfield. I have to admit that I was very excited and I was having a blast. When we returned to the apartment he said that he would "See me later." My mom then told me to go into her room and to close the door. I could not hear what they were talking about but they had a brief conversation and then he left.

My mother called me out of the room and sat me down. She said "Sean, that was your father." I was stunned. In my head, I was wondering why he didn't just tell me that himself, or why did she have to wait for my father to leave in order for her to tell me who he was. My speculation is that my mother wanted to reintroduce my father slowly back into my life and the handshake deal that they made was being put into play. However, it would be the last time that I would see my father for a couple of years.

I think after my father spent time with me, he wanted to take me and my mother was not having any of that, even if the courts had ordered it. For whatever reason, unbeknownst to me even today, my mother refused to give me over to my father at that time.

After my father's appearance, things began to unravel with my mother quickly. I began to spend a lot of time at other people's homes, friends of my mother's; she was purposely beginning to keep me away from Franklin Place (I'm sure she thought my father was going to snatch me away). The chess game between her and my father was again in full play surrounding me, and I believe that my mom was starting to deal with some personal demons as a result of her time with Mike who was no stranger to drugs. My new Camelot was coming to a horrible end, again!

Like in the past, I was suddenly packed up and taken away without saying goodbye to anyone. I could not believe that this was happening to me again. My mother, in her defiance of my father I believe, sent me away to a shelter. Or, her personal issues and finances were in such disarray that she just could not take care of me anymore and that sent me to the shelter. Either way, one thing was evident, she was not going to give me to my father. So, there I was, eight years old, alone, feeling betrayed and in a shelter for homeless children blaming myself. Why? Because I was never told why I was sent to the shelter in the first place; I just thought that I was not wanted anymore. I remember saying to myself, "what did I do wrong?" Yes, I blamed myself, again!

The "shelter" was now home! My mother was nowhere to be found again. All I could remember was being picked up at Franklin Place in Plainfield, NJ and being taken away suddenly by white people. I don't even remember telling my mother goodbye. Just try to imagine being snatched away from what you know and placed in a foreign place that was to become your home. I just could not believe that this was happening.

The shelter was very clean. The staff there was very courteous. This time I had my own bedroom. There were a lot of kids there, but we each had our own rooms. Breakfast, lunch, and dinner were run with military precision. We washed up before each meal, we each had our designated seats, and we weren't allowed to talk during meals. We all had our share of chores to do, and of course we had class to attend.

The kids there were a mix of all races. Everyone seemed to get along. I quickly made friends as we all shared a common thread of the situation; we were in a shelter for one reason or another. From what I can recall, and my mother refuses to discuss it with me, none of the kids there were waiting to be placed in foster homes. I remember the "recreation room" had a pool table and television. It was also where the phones were that the kids would be allowed to talk to their parents or guardians.

Discipline was dealt with in one of two ways: one, you were sent to your room or two, you would lose your television viewing time. If your chores were completed on time and you did not get in trouble, you were rewarded for good behavior by receiving extra television viewing time, not to extend past 9 pm. However, if you found yourself in trouble, you would find yourself going to bed with no television time. It was a simple leverage tool but very effective. You did not want to miss your television time because all the kids would talk about the different shows that came on.

They also awarded a "good kid of the week award;" it came with a little gold trophy. I craved that trophy, believing that if I won the award, my mother would come and get me because I had shown that I was a good kid. Well, I did eventually win the trophy and award, but my mother never showed up.

During my time at the shelter, I would sit for hours staring out of my bedroom window, hoping, praying, that my mother would come and pick me up. I didn't want to play with the other kids, nor did I want to socialize in the recreation room after a while. I would find myself sneaking down to the phone and lifting it up off the hook in hopes of hearing my mother's voice on the other end. In fact, I would sneak out of my room late night, knowing that I would get in trouble, and just sit by the phone hoping that my mother, or anyone for that matter, would call me.

The counselor on call would always find me after bed checks curled up on the floor asleep by the phone. It hurt me to watch the other children get phone calls while no one called for me, ever! I would hate to hear about the phone conversations from the other kids.

I really felt that I was the Bastard Child. There was so much racing through my little head, but the one thing I knew, I was alone!

I really began to become reclusive. Knowing what I know now, I was dealing with depression and rightfully so, but I was only eight. Winter came, and there was a barn that was right outside of my window, the same window that I would spend hours on end staring out of. Each time it snowed, I would see footprints leading from the barn to the building that I lived in. I had convinced myself that my mother had come and checked up on me while I was asleep, even though my room was on the second floor. Knowing that was not the case now, I really believed it then. I would literally break down and cry myself to sleep just about every night wondering what had I done to anyone to deserve this life?

One day a visitor finally came to visit me; it was my Aunt Cynthia, my mother's oldest sister. She also had my two cousins with her; I was so excited to see a relative. Although I knew who my Aunt and cousins were, I really hadn't spent that much time with them when I lived with Mike or on Franklin Place. But who cared? I was finally sitting down with someone that came to visit me and I finally felt loved. It was a one-time visit, but it was just what the doctor ordered.

My Aunt had a ton of questions she was asking me and I tried my best to answer them. They were the expected questions, like was I eating regularly, were they nice to me, was I getting along with the other kids in there? My honest answer to all was yes. I'm thinking sure, the place was fine but who wants to live in a shelter? Get me out of this place, Auntie!

When the visit came to a close, I remember seeing my Aunt begin to cry; she was hurt. I didn't understand why, but I knew one thing, I didn't want her or my cousins to leave. It would be the only time that anyone would come to visit me while I was living in the shelter. That included my grandmother, father, mother, uncles, other aunts etc. I even thought that my Aunt Cynthia would come back and get me to live with her seeing how hurt she was, but it was not to come. I'm not sure if the pain of it all was too much for my Aunt but again, she never returned to see me again. And all the while, the other kids were receiving regular visits; I sat alone. I would find out some years later that my Aunt actually tried to take me, but my mother said no. To this day I do not know why she said no.

The day came when I finally got a call from my mother. I was so happy to hear her voice. My smile was so electric that it could have lit up Las Vegas at night. However, it would be the only phone-call that I would receive at the shelter from my mother. Time stood still briefly, and I set aside the transgressions that had been levied against me by her hand. The call was brief, because I made it that way, and apparently she had found another apartment. She had told me about some of the local kids in the new neighborhood, but I just wanted to know one thing, when was she getting me out of the shelter? As she does now, or last we spoke, she carefully avoided the direct question. Tired of the disappointment, I simply dropped the phone and left it off the hook and walked away from it.

At that point I knew one thing, she had no idea when or if she was coming to get me. Once again, I felt abandoned by the one person who was supposed to love me unconditionally. Even now in my mid-forties I have no idea how long I was in that shelter, but it was no less than eight months to a year (which felt like an eternity). Although it was not the physical abuse that I had grown accustomed to; this time my frail psyche was a mess! And needless to say, mental abuse can be just as damaging, if not more harmful, than physical abuse.

I kept asking myself, why me? Why did I have to endure so much so young? Foolishly, I asked myself, did I piss God off? I remember thinking *what did I do to anyone to deserve this life?* At a young age, I began to wish that I were dead, especially after the mess that I was fed on the phone. In fact, there were times at the shelter when I seriously contemplated ending it all. I hated my life . . .

How could so much be placed on someone so young to bear? I was feeling like every bit the Bastard Child, scared and abandoned. I'm sure each of the other children in that shelter had their own crosses to carry, but I pray none of them had to endure what I had to by age eight. Life was truly brutal towards me. In fact, I think some adults may have given up on life if they had to endure what I had to up to that point.

Chapter 5

The New Kid on the Block

Now nine years of age, the time came when I was finally going to go back to live with my mother. She had found an apartment on Orange Place in Plainfield, New Jersey. When I made it to the apartment, I had my own room and not a couch to sleep on this time like our last apartment. It was bigger than the last apartment too, and it even had a hallway in it. Out of the window in my room, I could see the Bamberger's parking lot (Macy's). It also allowed me to see the back of what is known as "down town" Plainfield.

Plainfield, NJ, known as the Queen City and home of Olympian Milt Campbell and Parliament P-Funk, was known for its shopping district at the time. People would come from far and near just for the stores. Although the Newark riots had exacted a toll on Plainfield, the shopping district was still surviving. I had a bed and a dresser with a shelf and a little chair that was all mine. I even had my own television set in my bedroom. Apparently my mother had gotten her act together. She was working for "Manpower" on behalf of the city. My mother, a very intelligent woman, had the ability to work her way into any circle. I'm sure that acquiring the Manpower position was a breeze for her.

Financially, there seemed to be enough money in the home. There was also Rob, her live-in boyfriend. To Rob's credit he was a hard-working man, but my mother had total control of him. I guess this time she wanted a "yes man," no basket cases! Rob never beat me nor did anything to degrade me, but it took some time before I would open up to Rob; understandably I was guarded. And the one thing that I knew he would never do is try my mother; she was clearly in control of this relationship. Rob was your quintessential 9-to-5 meat and potatoes type of man. In fact, a good newspaper, dinner, followed by a television show and Rob was good-to-go for the night!

Trying to get adjusted to my new environment, the time came for me to go out into the neighborhood and meet some new friends. The other thing that I was going to have to face was being the new kid in school, Barlow School. My mother wanted me to meet Nick Stamboni, an Italian kid who lived across the hallway from me. He would be my first true friend in the neighborhood. He had two older brothers, Dom and Michael. His mother, Dorothy, had lived in Plainfield her entire life. She was a soft-spoken Italian woman but always had a nice smile and opened their home up to me. His father,

"Big Dom," was a throwback Italian man who hated me. A bigot by all accounts, he hated that his son had befriended me. Ironically, none of the children or the mother shared his bigotry. In fact, Dom and Michael were like older brothers to me. "Nicky" and I would remain tight for years to come. Truth be told, the Stamboni's were the ones who introduced me to Rock and Roll. Secretly, even to this day, I'm a closet *Kiss* fan because of them.

Nicky had two cousins who lived around the corner from our apartment complex, David and Tommy Blanken's. They rounded out the initial crew on my block. Their mother Elemi was the Kool-Aid mom of the neighborhood. She would eventually become my babysitter as my mother was working religiously. A mean cook, I looked forward to having dinner at the Blanken's. Like her sister, Dorothy, she treated me like one of her own. Unlike Big Dom, her husband Tom had some soul to him. To hear Tom talk, you would've swore he was Black. Like being a closet Kiss fan thanks to the Stamboni's, Elemi had turned me into a lover of Italian food. I love Soul Food, but there's nothing like a good Italian dish!

The building I lived in was managed and run by Mr. Cerrito (who was Nicky, David, and Tommy's Grandfather). He was an actual immigrant from Italy—hot tempered, spoke with his hands, and hated kids. We would think of ways to torment him just out of fun. As a crew, we were tight! It came to pass that we found ourselves staying the night at each other homes almost every weekend, outside of me being black, you would of thought we were brothers. When you saw one of us, you saw all of us, always together.

At that time, HBO was a novelty and the Blanken's had cable at their house. Nicky and I would crash at the Blanken's just to watch the late-night Rated R movies where HBO would at times have movies that showed "boobies." To a bunch of adolescent boys, that was heaven; it just did not get any better than that. The trick was we just had to stay up late enough to catch a rated R movie and not get caught by Elemi. Yes, times were good then. Dave and Tommy even had an Atari, a novelty to me because we did not have Atari at the shelter, but I caught on quick. A big bag of Doritos, a 2-Liter Pepsi, and nothing but time, we would have at the Atari all day and night . . .

As we ate dinner at each other's house on a regular basis, there was one time in particular when I had dinner at Nicky's house. Not

35

that it was something new, but this time, for the first time, Big Dom (Nicky's father) was there. I remember we had steak. Sitting at the table everything appeared to be just fine. In fact, I rather enjoyed sitting at the table with Nicky's father; I thought he finally accepted me as Nicky's friend. After I ate dinner, I went back across the hall to my apartment. About an hour or so later Nicky was knocking on the door; he was crying. Apparently his father absolutely lost it when I left. What I thought was an innocent dinner was anything but. I asked Nicky what happened and he said that his father had told his mother in a very harsh way that as long as he lived, there better not ever be another nigger sitting at his dinner table! Nicky being a kid felt ashamed to tell my mother and me. My mother thanked Nicky and said she would take care of it, and boy did she!

For the first time in my life, racism had greeted me. My mother, filled with rage, went on the hunt for Mr. Stamboni. He had left the apartment and gone to his favorite watering hole, the Bridge Tavern in North Plainfield, NJ; but that did not stop my mother. She wanted blood! So off to the "Bridge" she went. Big Dom was not at the bar after all, but his son "little Dom" was there. My mother unleashed her wrath on little Dom in his place. She grabbed a pool stick and broke it over the pool table and dared Dom to call her a nigger and wanted to know where his coward father was. Little Dom, an innocent victim in this case, did his best to calm my mother down.

She single-handedly shut the bar down that night according to the stories. Once home, my mother said that I was not allowed to go over to Nicky's anymore. My mother eventually did apologize to Little Dom for exploding on him but she had a point to make and it manifested on him. Knowing my mother, had she caught up with Big Dom that initial night, he would have caught a bad one. I guess karma is a beast; some years later, Dorothy would leave Big Dom for an African American. Go figure! In time, my mom would eventually let me go back over to Nicky's. I'm sure it was after she finally caught up and dealt with the right Dom.

As I got to know the other kids on the neighboring blocks, my circle of friends got bigger. There were the Smith's—Raymond, Joey, Daemon, and David. There were the Crawford's—Suzette, Camille, Stevie, and Chris. They had the house with the manicured lawn and a no-nonsense father. Their mom, like the other moms in the neighborhood, allowed the kids in the neighborhood to come over to the house. I remember how clean the Crawford's home was. I was almost scared to walk on the carpet. When it came to tackle football, the Crawford's backyard was it; it was Super Bowl Sunday every time we played there.

Everyone seemed to get along well as kids. However, in each neighborhood, a bully must reside. Our neighborhood bully was Stan. Stan, plain and simple, was a big and massive kid. We seemed like infants compared to Stan. In addition to having to deal with Stan, there was Daniel, my personal nemesis. Daniel and I just did not hit it off. Rounding out the neighborhood was the McKinney's—Victor, Randy, Ali, and all the sisters, oh, and the neighborhood pit-bull terrier, Champ. Randy was a year older than me; but without question Randy was the neighborhood big brother to everyone.

In time, as the rhythm of the neighborhood was unfolding, Stan became a serious issue. His mother, a tough woman in her own right, was not one to mess with either. Stan was exacting his toll on the neighborhood and no matter how many times you told his mother, it just didn't seem to matter; in fact I think it fueled his bullying. Daily he would pick anyone of us to, for lack of a better term, beat up.

It got to be the case where none of us wanted to go outside and play for fear of Stan, and I mean no one! It even got to be the case where we would secretly meet up just to avoid running into him. How could someone so young be so mean? It would be a few years later but Stan eventually went to jail for stabbing someone. Yes, that was the mess that I was dealing with at nine. Just when I really thought the physical abuse was over in the home, I was beginning to experience beef in the street.

The day came when Stan would unleash on me; for whatever reason, he chose to "up the ante." Not only did he beat me up that day but he also chose to drive his foot into the middle of my back with all his might. As I laid on the ground, I remember that I couldn't move my arms or legs. I really thought that I was paralyzed; none of the kids could help me because most of the kids were scared of Stan. Eventually I regained the movement of my extremities. Muddied, I made my way home, David and Nicky by my side. I stumbled into my mother's apartment. Horrified, my mother could see that I was hurt bad. She asked me what had happened and I told her exactly what happened. Stan's muddy footprint was squarely stained in my back.

My mother was once again enraged; shortly thereafter she was out the door and on her way to deal with Stan and his mother. When she returned she said that I would not be having any more problems with Stan. I was relieved; Stan was no joke! Stan never did bully me again after that, but he still exacted his hand on the neighborhood. However, that would be just the beginning of the many battles to come on Orange Place.

Daniel "G" was my other nemesis, one of three during my time on Orange Place. We were equal in size. Daniel, an original West End kid, lived next door to the Smith's. For his age, he had a lot of responsibilities. He took care of this younger brother Thomas and his little sister. His mother was a nice lady as well, like the bulk of the moms in the neighborhood. Daniel, when he had time, would play with the rest of us in the neighborhood. Although his time was short, he made the most of the time he had to play and would always leave way before the streetlights came on like the rest of us.

It seemed like no matter what game we played, whether it was football, baseball, tag, hide and seek, anything, Daniel and I were on opposing sides. We would argue back and forth, but unlike Stan, he was my size and I didn't fear Daniel. The back-and-forth would go on for a while. Of course the other kids in the neighborhood would amp us up to fight one another but up until that time, we hadn't fought.

When Daniel's cousins would come over to stay the night from the West End (the rougher side of town), it got really nasty between us. Daniel would talk tough and I knew I was outnumbered up to that point. I would go in the house telling myself "One day I'm going to catch him at the right time and it's on!" I just knew I was going to teach him a lesson. Well, finally the time came when I was going to show him; it was time to "get it in." I went to his house by myself and invited him outside and said let's fight; yes, just like that. He told me he would be right back and when he opened the door we went into the middle of the gravel parking lot where he lived and got it in. Looking back I should have waited to catch him away from his house. I'm sure he told his mother I came there to fight him and she said you better go out there and whoop his behind!

It was winter at the time and we squared off in the snow. I threw the first punch and it landed flush. The front door of his house opened up and his mother said, "you better not lose." After that it was all downhill for me. If it was on a Ten-Point system like in boxing, after my first blow, he won the remaining rounds on all cards. I had to chalk up the loss. I didn't mind losing and my mother was proud of me for standing and fighting given the ordeal of Stan. We were good to go after that; I think we gained a mutual respect for one another. But from that initial fight, I was slowly learning how to give and take a punch and to face a threat in the streets.

My third nemesis at that time was a duo of brothers. The older brother was much bigger of the two. They lived a few blocks over from mine. Unfortunately my mother had a bad smoking habit and it seemed like at least once daily I would find myself walking to the store to get her a pack of cigarettes. Ben Franklin Liquors was the store that I went to most of the time to get my mom's cigarettes and it was on Front Street in Plainfield, NJ right up the street from the two brother's house (i.e., in their neighborhood).

Call it bad luck, but I would always run into the two brothers at the store, as it also served as the local arcade to a degree. Depending on the encounter, I would either get beat up by the younger brother or chased home by him and his older brother. Either way, I hated to go to the store. It even got to be the case that I would go to the Red Carpet Deli to get my mom's cigarettes in North Plainfield, NJ; I would do anything to avoid those two. There were times I was getting chased home by them and I just made it into my apartment hallway glass doors. In fact, I was surgeon-like with getting my key out of my pocket and opening the door to avoid them.

I would lie in my room at night and I would wonder why I had to deal with so much, why did the two brothers feel the need to single me out; maybe because I was small in size for my age? Maybe because I was the new kid on the block, who knew? Some nights I would just lay there in my bed for hours until I would fall asleep, just to be awaked by one of my night terror episodes (no they hadn't gone away). Even when I would knock on my mom's bedroom door for comfort, she would "go off" on me and tell me to "take me behind back to bed!" It felt like the world was collapsing in on me, again!

The only comfort I would take during the night would actually be the delivery trucks making their stops at the various downtown stores in the morning. I would lie there awake in my bed many nights until I heard the sound of those trucks, which for some reason gave me a sense of comfort. It would be only then that I would fall asleep, just briefly, before I would have to go to school.

With each new day came the routine challenges (night terrors, bullies, and staying awake all night); they were staples in my life at this point but it was better than living in that shelter alone. Like with Daniel, I knew I was going to have to deal with the two brothers' somehow. It would be by chance that I would own up to the challenge. In the neighborhood, all the boys would play football as mentioned, first in the back of the Crawford's yard if we could, or behind the bank across the street from Ben Franklin's liquor in Plainfield, NJ; that meant there was a good chance of me running into the two brothers. Well, as luck would have it, we ended up playing football behind the bank this day. Up to this point, I had not run into the brothers there as we had played football games there many times before. As the law of averages would have it, this day would be the day where I would be forced to stand and fight, my luck had run out again.

Out of nowhere, my worst fears had come to pass; the two brothers were approaching the field and I had no place to run and no means of escape. Randy McKinney, who was there that day, saw the fear in my eyes and told me "You better not run!" He knew that the two brothers were notorious for chasing me home, and that they were not coming to play football (they never had in the past).

Randy told the oldest brother as they approached the field that nobody was going to jump me and if there was going to be a fight, it would be a one-on-one fight. Randy being my security blanket from the older brother, I knew I would get a fair fight (the older brother respected Randy). All the kids in the neighborhood were there, except Stan, and they circled us inside of them. My heart pounding, I knew it was either going to be him or me. As we started to fight he caught me with a few good punches. However, I was still reluctant to hit him back as I feared the payback later on by his big brother if I won the fight. Randy said, "Don't be scared, I got your back" so I threw my first punch. The younger brother slipped my punches and I knew I was in trouble. I had to think fast on my feet.

When he went to throw his next few punches I did the only thing that I felt would help me out, I tackled him to the ground. There on the ground, he became a fish out of water. I was able to pin his shoulders down and punch him in the face a few times. He eventually got me off of him and we were once again on our feet squared off; however, this time my confidence was with me a little. Immediately he threw another punch feeling that he had the advantage of the fistfight by being on his feet. I ducked his punch and I was able to get him into a Full Nelson. From there I drug him over to the nearest car and started hitting his head against the vehicle. His brother ran over to help, but true to his word, Randy did not let the older brother jump in.

When I finally let go of the younger brother he slid down the car and to the ground. Randy and the other kids said "run," and run I did. After I left, the ambulance had to be called and the younger brother had to be taken to the hospital. Later on that day Randy came over to the apartment to tell my mother and me what had happened after I left. I had told my mother what had happened but I guess coming from Randy it gave her a sense of the complete picture. My mother did not say anything else to me about the fight after that.

Strangely in the neighborhood I had gained some acceptance. The tide had turned for the better for me on Orange Place after that fight (and many, if not all of those friendships still exist today). I never had another fight on the block again thank God, because at that time I was no fighter. When the eventual time came when I would see the two brothers again at Ben Franklin Liquors, it would be different. This time I got a head nod and an accepting "what-up" at the store and that was it. Inside I was praying that they did not jump me, but I really believe Randy having my back at the bank that day put things in order for everyone. Bottom line, it was a fair fight, the result of a good old-fashioned back-in-the-day fistfight, a page that many should take note of as violent gun crimes now ravage our inner cities. Lord knows Daniel kicked my butt that day I went to his house.

With all my nemeses of Orange Place put to rest (for now) it was on to just being a kid. As my neighborhood dilemma came to a close, one was starting to grow for Randy . . . Stan! Although my mother insured that Stan would no longer be a factor in my life, Randy was now the object of Stan's bullying. Randy, more than capable of handling his own with his hands, was soon to square off with Stan. As it would come to be, Stan held the neighborhood in terror. Nobody wanted to be around him; he made for some long days for a lot of kids in the neighborhood. It was not a question of if Stan would beat you up, but when was your turn. I really hated Stan with all my heart, but I was now safe. Although we were basically all the same age, Stan was so much bigger than everyone else in the neighborhood. Simply put, nobody could beat him on the block, he was the "Duke" of the block, or so we thought!

It was a typical summer day and we were playing touch football in the street. That day all of the kids of the neighborhood were out taking part. Not only were the boys playing football but the girls of the neighborhood were out too. It would set the stage for a shift in the neighborhood that would finally set things right amongst us all regarding Stan. As the football game unfolded, none other than Stan came walking up the street. Stan had wanted to know why he was not invited to play football. Nobody would speak up; naturally we were all scared to say anything.

Stan, not happy at all took the football. Randy said, "Stan, give the ball back." Stan replied, "This ball is mine." Randy, now a little more brazen, said, "You are going to give the football back." Stan immediately took that as a sign of disrespect from Randy. As the rest of us sat back terrified to say anything, Randy was growing more and more confident by the second. Inside I was saying to myself, "Give him some 'act right' Randy." Yes, I was tough inside, but my exterior dare not show it. The circle was starting to form around Randy and Stan and the fight was about to be on! Ali, Randy's younger brother tried to get Randy to go into the house, but Randy would have nothing of it. He was tired of Stan as all of us were.

Randy would serve as our avenger that day. Randy knew that if he lost the fight against Stan that day we were all in trouble. As I had faced my demons earlier regarding the two brothers from a few blocks over, which Randy was there for, maybe Randy was saying to himself that it was time for him to face the demon of our neighborhood.

Stan took off his shirt and said, "what's up." Randy said "what's up with you?" They began to circle each other; I know Stan really did not believe that Randy was going to actually stand up and fight him, but Randy was very serious. His younger brother Ali watched with fear, as we all did. Randy was the big brother to us all in the neighborhood. Once Stan realized that Randy was serious he treated it as such. He caught Randy with a punch, and his lip was busted immediately, but it seemed to only fuel Randy. The determination in Randy's eyes was undeniable. Stan caught him again and again with punches and Randy did what he could not to fall to his knees.

Randy, dazed, must have said to himself, "today is my day!" After all, he took Stan's best and was still standing. It was Randy's turn; he threw a punch and it connected. Stan was stunned, in trouble off of the one punch. We all could tell that Randy was determined. Randy began to punch Stan again and again in the face. It was as if Randy said to himself *if I stop punching, Stan is going to get the upper hand.*

Once we realized that Randy was winning the fight, we too became more vocal, screaming, Randy, get him! Randy would not be denied that day; when the fight was over, Stan wanted no more parts of Randy. Randy, breathing heavy, knew he had been in a fight that day but he was the victor. Stan, defeated, grabbed his shirt and headed back home. Inside I said to myself, handle that Stan!

Randy was simply the neighborhood hero after that. I asked Randy once he caught his breath if he was scared and he said, "Man, yeah, that's why I kept punching," as he sported a devilish smile on his face and gave me a reassuring wink. In the days and weeks to come in the neighborhood, Stan never messed with any of us ever again. Randy by his own hand had made it safe for us all to be kids.

Throughout my years living on Orange Place, school was pretty straightforward for me. Sure, I had my share of schoolyard fights, as did any other kid growing up, but nothing traumatic. I even found myself placing another permanent scar on my opposite eyebrow in school as I ran into a door when one of my classmates was coming through it and I was trying to go through it simultaneously. I would find myself a bit of a loner at lunch and after school.

At times, I would walk home by myself along the Brook in North Plainfield, NJ behind Barlow School to avoid kids. Psychologically, I was still dealing with a lot of challenges that children at my age should not have had to deal with. Trying to make sense of it all, I would find myself being guarded, even at school. But something was becoming evident to me, school and learning was a natural thing for me; I was discovering that I was book smart (when I applied myself) and in the years to come it would prove to be my saving grace.

During this time, my mother held a job and was able to afford me a few things that I had not been exposed to before. I was able to attend Camp Speers Eljabra in Pennsylvania. I attended the camp for a few years during the summer and it made for a great time. In fact, the camping experience is one of my fonder memories of my childhood. During this time, I learned that I had other brothers and a sister on the West End of town. My father, who was absent from my life at this point, had again resurfaced. He was again attempting to establish a relationship with me, but I really did not know him at all.

My mother up to this point had not told me that I had any other siblings in regards to my father. My father (in his efforts to have all his children know one another) brought my brothers and sister to my mother's apartment. I was very excited to know that I had other brothers and a sister, but at the same time I was confused because I really did not know my father. In part, I was getting to know my father and my siblings at the same time, a lot to take in at such a young age.

To his credit, my father from that point on would remain a fixture in my life; he would battle fiercely to put me under his roof. That aside, I enjoyed the fact that I had brothers and sisters in New Jersey and I wanted to get to know them, as well as them wanting to get to know me. There was Guy, Kirk, Lynn, and my oldest brother Darrow.

My brothers and sister stayed with my grandmother on the West End of town but I had yet to go down to that end of town to meet her. The West End was and still is considered the rougher part of Plainfield, New Jersey. Up to that time, I was not allowed to go past Park Avenue, which served as an unofficial boundary for me not to cross by my mother. My brothers were brought by to spend time with me as we got to know one another; I soon discovered that my oldest brother was very well known on the West End.

My brother Darrow, as fate would have it, was one of the toughest kids on that end of town. He was the "Stan" of not only a particular block, but of the West End. Yes, there were other tough kids down on that side of town, but Darrow was definitely one of the toughest! I remember Randy finding out that "Darrow Brown" was my brother and just not believing it. It would take Darrow coming down to my mother's house for him to finally believe it.

Darrow was a man-child by any standard at that time, and as tough as the day was long. However, behind closed doors, he was a very caring, loving, and protective brother. I, in contrast, was small and frail and all but reveled in the fact that I had a "Stan" as my brother.

My grandmother on the West End was a no-nonsense woman who worked at the police station and ran a tight ship; I learned quickly that "Nana" was a loving woman but no joke! My grandfather, "Pop-Pop" was a tall gentleman, and my father adored him greatly. I envied the relationship that my father had with his father. Truth be told, it's probably why my father fought so hard to keep his kids all together.

Now age eleven, my mother had lost her job. Things started to once again unravel for me. Having moved on from her original position with the city, she was working for Federal Express and was terminated. Rob, her live-in boyfriend, held down a factory job but he did not make enough to pay all of the bills in the apartment; something had to give. That something was me, and once again I was sent packing, but this time it would be with my father. However, before my mother would relinquish me to my father, she sent me to stay with "Cootie."

Who was Cootie? She was a southern woman with a heart of gold who had moved up north to live at some point in her life. She was one of my mother's best friends in Plainfield, NJ and I was no stranger to her home. To this day I love Cootie like a second mother. So how did my mother go about letting me know I would be staying with Cootie? She simply packed up my clothes and told me that I would be staying the weekend with her. Well, that weekend turned out to be months. This time, as I was a little older, I was able to deal with it to a degree. I did, however, find myself sitting on Cootie's porch for days and hours on end once again waiting for my mother to come and get me.

Cootie's children Viola, Kenny, Mitchell, Rose, and Yvette treated me just like a brother. My mother had once again moved me without telling my father because I didn't see him at all while I lived with Cootie. I'm sure that added to the bitter feud between them regarding my custody. Eventually my mother came back to get me, but it had been months. Where had she been? Something was different about my mother; she really was not the same. Cootie, who had become like a surrogate mother to me, would call my mother's apartment from time-to-time and check up on me once I returned to live with my mother, maybe sensing that something was not right.

Money became an issue, I started to notice that my piggy bank (literally) was being emptied, and the money that I had collected as a Boy Scout for a fundraiser had turned up missing. I didn't have an answer for the Boy Scouts when it was time to turn the money in, but I knew where the money had gone. In tough times, I guess people do what they have to do, but I was bearing that cross and I never went back to the scouts after that because I was so embarrassed.

Knowing what I know now, I know exactly what was driving the change in my mother. I knew she was not the same and it would be brutally played out on me. Mitchell, Cootie's son, had come to stay the night at the apartment. Luck would have it that we went into the downstairs area of Bamberger's where all the video games were at and played video games for hours. Having lost track of time and Mitchell being older, I thought we were fine. Eventually I told Mitchell we had to go and he agreed.

By the time we had arrived back to the apartment, which was literally 50 yards behind Bamberger's, my mother had called the police and Cootie was at the apartment. My mother had reported us missing, but honestly we were only gone for a few hours. In the past I had stayed outside way longer than that. Paranoia, I believe, had set in and my mother had over-reacted. Once the police knew we were okay, they departed, along with Cootie and Mitchell. My mother had told Cootie that it was best that she take Mitchell home.

Feeling that I had not done anything wrong, I did not think that my mother was going to react, but I was wrong! Once my mother knew that the apartment was clear, she came into my room. She said, "Sean I'm going to beat you because you embarrassed me." I was saying to myself, no you are paranoid! But that eerie familiar tone of violence like Amelia was resonating through her words to me, "I'm going to beat you!" She shut the bedroom door and I braced myself for another brutal beating at the hands of someone who supposedly "loved me!" Thinking that she was going to use the belt, mentally I knew I could tough it out; I think she knew it too because she didn't grab a belt this time, instead, she pulled the extension cord out of the wall to beat me with.

When she began to beat me with the extension cord, the pain was so indescribable that emotionally it still makes my hair on my arms stand on end as I write about it. The cord ripped into my skin, I only had my underwear on and I did everything I could to protect myself. I laid in the fetal position realizing that she had torn a gash into my side from the extension cord. I was bleeding badly. Afraid to let her see the blood, I turned and laid on the side that I was bleeding from and balled up as tight as I could until the beating stopped, keeping the blood pool beneath me. In her fury, she didn't realize that I was bleeding. Yet, this was the woman who "loved me;" what was the point behind it all? Who knows, but a heavy price was paid . . .

She left me on the floor and left out of the room. I stayed there for a while until I was able to move knowing that she would come in and check on me eventually. Afraid that she would get mad at me and beat me some more, I quickly changed my underwear that had the blood on it and cleaned the floor up with them. I stuffed the bloody underwear in a racetrack box that I kept under my bed until I could throw the underwear away without being caught. I hid the wound from my mother, scared of what she might do to me if she found out; putting tissue on the wound daily until it healed. To this day I bear a scar on my right hip from that day. I guess she taught me a lesson that I already had a PhD in, getting the life beat out of me!

One thing was evident—my mother was changing, for the worse! It's not like she had not beaten me before, but unlike accidentally smashing my nose when I was younger, this time she meant to hurt me, to make a point, whatever that was? I had never been beaten by my mother with an extension cord before that and I just could not believe what she had done. I again found myself terrified in my own confines and I did not recognize my own mother anymore. Whatever vice that was taking hold of my mother would hold her soul for years to come. Sadly, it would set into motion more years of disappointment, heartache, and pain for a little boy now a pre-teen.

Chapter 6

Guess Who's Coming to Dinner

The day came when my mother's house of cards finally came crashing down and I did not understand what was going on. She was taking all of my clothes out of the closet and drawers and placing them into a plastic bag. Confused, I asked my mother if she was taking me somewhere again to stay for a while. I remember her telling me to "Go sit down somewhere!" I knew after that, I was going somewhere for a long time. Nervous and reluctant, I tried again to get it out of my mother where I'd be going, but she acted as if I was not there. It was at that point that I knew my mother had lost the apartment.

In my mind, I was praying that I did not have to go back to the shelter! Or even worse, I did not want to go back to Florida. But rest assured I was on my way out from Orange Place. Once again there were no goodbyes to my friends, it was simply my plastic bags thrown into her car and we headed towards the opposite side of town.

Now heading towards the West End, I anxiously held my breath at every stop, not knowing where we were going. When the car finally pulled over, we were at my grandmother and grandfather's house on West 5th street (on my father's side). My mom told me to get out of the car and wait while she went into the house. Shortly thereafter, my father came out of the house and told me to get my stuff. My mother walked right past me without showing any emotions; inside, *I was like what is going on?* She got in her car and pulled off with no goodbye, no I'll be back, no reassuring hug, just gone! I was finally at the doorstep of my father.

All I knew is that once again I'd be thrust upon a situation that I would have to deal with by my mother's hand. As she got into her car without really looking at or saying anything to me, I again blamed myself for the situation. Why? Who knows, but by that time I was a wreck inside. However, I did know one thing—as she pulled off, I knew she was not coming back for me anytime soon.

The time spent with my father's side of the family allowed me to get to know my cousins and many relatives associated with that side of the family. My family included the Cox's of the East End, the Doyle's, Hamilton's, Brown's, and of course all of the Lilly's. I was actually happy to know that I had plenty of relatives in the town I called home. My grandmother on my father's side in the years to come would turn out to be one of my best friends and biggest supporters in my life. I must also mention that my Aunt Cynthia (on my mother's side) would also play a crucial role in my life, as I became a man. But back to my father . . .

Although me, my brothers, and sister stayed with my grandparents on 5th street, my father had actually bought a home on West 4th street and he had planned on moving us all in there with his girlfriend Bunny and her daughter Mecca (they would marry some years later). Used to moving by now, I planned for the eventual move. It would be months before the house was ready for us to move into, but that summer all the boys would go over to the house to help in the preparation. Truth-be-told, I hated fixing up that house, but it made me gain an appreciation for honest hard work as my father paid us for our efforts.

The previous owner, Mr. Money, was well known on the west side of town and he had left all types of news clippings in the house when he moved out. Me being the secret bookworm that I was, I found myself intrigued about the articles that were in the paper about him. My father would yell at me and tell me to "get back to cleaning," but as I did I would continue to secretly read the clippings during my breaks. I felt like the house was a piece of history in Plainfield.

When the time came to go back to school, my father kept me in Maxson middle school on the East End of Plainfield, NJ. He would take me in the mornings and pick me up after school. As I lived with my mother during my seventh grade year in Maxson, it was time for the eighth grade. I knew I had to keep my grades tight as my father was not one to play games when it came to tightening up his boys with the belt; I would learn that lesson the hard way when I received my report card and it was not good. I knew what was to come once my father took a look at it. Strangely my father did not beat me right away and I actually thought that I had gotten away with it. Inside I was telling myself that it could not be "this easy." My confidence grew and I acted as if everything was okay, even chumming up with my father a little. He gave no signs that he had plans to discipline me at all.

As I recall, by a saving grace (or so I thought) my mother out of nowhere was at my grandparent's house to take me back. I could not believe what was happening. I was happy to see my mother, but I knew I had dodged a bigger bullet in my father, or so I thought! As my mother told me to get my things, I was telling my brothers and sisters goodbye and packed all my stuff up into garbage bags again. My father told me he needed to see me upstairs before I left so I thought he just wanted to tell me goodbye in private. However, that was not the case and my father wanted to beat me before I left because of my report card. Up to that point I had never been disciplined by my father, I just heard about it from my brothers. Knowing that my mother was down stairs waiting on me, I knew that [it] would be over quick.

My father sitting on the upstairs bed called me upstairs to him and told me to take my pants off! He was methodical in his discipline, he told me to look forward and to put my hands out as if I was pushing against an imaginary wall, he then told me to bend my knees, as he spoke to me as to why he was beating me; my mind flashed back to the years of physical abuse that I had already endured unbeknownst to him. I was saying to myself, not again!

As the belt struck me, the pain radiated throughout my body. My father was heavy handed and he was making a point to show me that he meant business. What my father did not know is that with each stroke of the belt I was reliving a horrible nightmare at the expense of a so-called loved one again. I know my father hadn't been a part of my life back then, so he could not have known about the previous abuse because I know he would have killed Mike and Amelia. Mentally I was saying to myself, I wonder if my father knows why my grades were bad, that I was a wreck inside.

When my father finished beating me, I tried to pick myself up off of the floor but my legs gave out. In fact, I couldn't walk for a few minutes; I was hurt badly again! Once I finally collected myself I had to go down stairs and face my siblings, knowing they just heard me catch a serious beating upstairs. My mother and father (who had made his way downstairs after the beating) were arguing and I knew my mother was taking me no matter what my father said. As they went back and forth arguing, I asked my brother Guy to take a look and my back side to see if there was any blood, and he said "no but your butt is throbbing and I can see it." We still joke about it today but when it actually happened back then it wasn't too funny.

I remember putting my bags into the car and asking myself, "where now?" What just happen to me? Up to this point I kept all of my pain inside, not wanting to let anyone know how I felt and that I hated life at this point. As my mother drove off from 5th street, I knew we were leaving Plainfield, but where were we going now?

The next place that I would call home was my Aunt Cynthia's, the same aunt that came to visit me at the shelter years before. She lived in Edison, NJ off of Stelton Road. My two cousins lived there along with my Uncle James (by common-law marriage). My Uncle James was a distinguished gentleman that only drove Cadillac's, and was as smooth as the day was long. He treated me just like family, sometimes letting me play on his CB Radio and yes, even letting me handle the 8-Track from time to time, that was serious because he didn't let anyone touch his car.

My cousins grew up pretty sheltered from what I had experienced. Edison, NJ at the time did not have a lot of African Americans and their mannerisms were even reflective of their environment. My cousin Vicky and I would remain thick as thieves for years until adulthood. I had stayed at my aunt's house quite a few times as a kid (after the shelter) and I felt very comfortable in her home. Like I mentioned before, my aunt actually became one of, if not, the biggest supporters of me as I became a man.

Knowing that my aunt stayed in an apartment, there was not a lot of room for my mother and I, so where would we lay our heads? Once we got settled into the apartment my mother told me to take my things into the basement. I said "the basement?" My mother said yes, that's where our new home is going to be. I remember turning on the lights as I headed down to the basement as saying to myself God watch over me, please.

Still hurting from the beating at my father's hand, I made my way down stairs to set my things down. The basement was somewhat of a finished basement but all of our things were down there. My mom had placed some large oval throw rugs on the floor and had divided the basement into makeshift rooms by placing her long dresser and mirror in between us. My bed was on the far side with my dresser on the backside of my mothers. My mother had transformed the basement into our apartment off of Orange Place. I just took a deep breath and knew that this would be home for a while.

Naturally I would have to go to school in Edison and I was dreading that day. Unlike my cousins, I did not grow up there so I did not know anyone outside of them. However, I did know one thing—I was not going to take any mess from the white boys, after all I was from Plainfield and I had to represent, or so I thought, right? Well the day finally arrived when I had to go to school. My mom registered me and I got my schedule from my guidance counselor. In those days the styles in Plainfield, NJ included Puma, Nike Cortez, Spalding, and Kangaroo sneakers, Gloria Vanderbilt, Lee's, Devil Jeans and Kangol hats, but not in Edison; I immediately stood out like a sore thumb.

My cousin Anita I think was more embarrassed to have me in school with her, as we were the same age. I would have thought she would at least take me under her wing and say "hey, this is my cousin Sean," but it was anything but. She kept her distance from me in school, as if we were not even related. Why? Who knows? This was the same cousin that I was living with every day. At lunch, I could have been on the moon for all that mattered, as I was the new kid and of course no one wanted to sit or have anything to do with me. In fact, no one really tried to make friends with me at all! And yes I tried to make friends but it was not to be. Unlike Maxson School in Plainfield where I knew everyone, this was the polar opposite.

As the days, weeks, and months passed, I fell back to the one gift I knew I had when I applied myself, books. But socially I was becoming an outsider in a school where I was one of a few African Americans in the entire 8th grade. Kids being kids, I started to become the object of their attention in a negative way. I was the butt of racial jokes, called nigger and spear chucker, and felt totally outnumbered; racism was again making its way into my life. The anger that was inside of me was incredible, but I knew if I lashed out as a black student, an outsider, in a predominantly white school, it was all downhill for me. I bit my tongue for months and the other kids took that as a sign of weakness.

Although I had told my mother about what was going on at school, she told me to try and make friends. I said "Mom, those kids do not like me because I'm black," but she was not hearing it. She didn't want to make any waves at my aunt's house; we had nowhere else to go and she was not going to give me back to my father. Again, I felt trapped and that my back was against the wall. That said, I knew what I had to do and I would carry through on my thoughts, even if it would cost me another beating.

The day came when I had enough of the ridicule. I was cornered in the gym locker room and taunted by a group of boys, but this time I did not bite my tongue or turn the other cheek. I said to the one kid with the biggest mouth, "why don't we settle this after school."

He looked at his friend and said, "After school then!" As the day progressed, the word spread amongst the other students that there was going to be a fight. My cousin Anita even came up to me and asked me if the rumors were true. I said yes, and I'm going to fight the boy after school. My cousin was actually mad at me for the fight. Not that I was getting picked on, but that I was embarrassing her. I said to myself, really? Thanks for standing by my side cousin! I did know one thing—if I lost the fight, it would make life impossible for me in that school.

With the time approaching, it seemed like every kid in the school knew about the fight but the teachers. When the final school bell rang, everyone raced out to the parking lot by the public library to see the spectacle. Of course the kid that I was supposed to fight had the backing of the entire school as I was viewed as an outsider. Alone, I walked up with my books with no one in my corner. I sat my books down and we were quickly circled in. My cousin Anita chose not to show up; any support would have helped in that moment . . . any! Me and the other boy squared off on each other, he was bigger (chubby) so I know he thought he had the advantage. He rushed me, trying to use his weight. I sidestepped him and he missed me. Embarrassed, I could see his rage growing. I was just looking for a break from the tormenting and this kid had no idea how much physical punishment I could endure.

When he rushed me again, I immediately put him into a headlock. Firmly planted, I rode him to the ground. The crowd was quiet and I began to punch him in the face over and over again. The position that I had him in didn't allow him to gain the advantage. The crowd became quiet; the point was made and in an instant the fight was over. I let him up and his nose was bloody. I asked him "is it over?" He didn't say anything but I could tell in his eyes that we were done. The crowd broke up and miraculously some of the kids even picked my books up for me and handed them to me.

When I got home my mother and my aunt were waiting at the dining room table, my cousin had "sold me out," and she said that I was a troublemaker at school. I told my cousin, my aunt, and my mother that I was not from Edison and that I hated it there and that I was not a trouble maker; I couldn't allow the other kids to continue to call me a nigger and pick on me just because I was black. However, my mother knew that I had spoken to her about this already so she played along because it was now on her doorstep. Knowing I had to stand up for myself, nothing really happened to me at home. My mom knew I had been dealing with some serious bigotry with the kids at school so I got a pass.

Looking back, I do know the right thing to do was to let the school administration know about the badgering and bullying, but at the time I handled it the best way I knew how. There was no "anti-bullying" campaign in place for me during that time like there is today. When I returned to school the next day, people began to speak to me in the halls. It was weird; in just 24 hours, my life had turned for the better somewhat at school. Lunch was still a challenge but at least the kids were speaking to me now. Eventually even the kid that I got into the fight with began to speak to me.

Ironically there were three black kids (my peers) that I tried to befriend but they had lived in Edison for quite some time and they wanted no part of me, being from Plainfield. The one time that I did have them over to my aunt's apartment, they asked where my bedroom was so we could go hang out in there. Not thinking much of it I took them into the basement where I stayed. When they got down there I remember one of them asking me "you live in the basement?" I said "yes!" They looked at one another strangely, and I could not make out what the big deal was. I forgot that they had a more "privileged life" in Edison, so this was beneath them and it showed immediately. I never asked anyone to come over again while we lived in that basement. Truth be told, I really didn't have that many friends to begin with while living in Edison; I was ignored by them after that, even asking me what I wanted when I came around. So much for the argument of "birds of a feather . . ."

Across the hall lived Mr. Simmons; he had roots in Plainfield and he had two daughters and a son. Mr. Simmons' apartment was nice and he opened the doors for the kids that lived in his building when his kids were visiting. In fact, while in the six grade he was my football coach while I played for the Eagles as part of the Sportsman League in Plainfield. He owned an exterminator company and was quite successful as a business owner. He always gave sound advice and I looked up to him. But my admiration for him was dwarfed by my first puppy love in life, his daughter Nicky.

Nicky was beautiful by all accounts; her eyes were lightly colored and although we were just kids, she was breathtaking, stunning! Her hair was wavy and she always wore it in a ponytail. If this was "puppy love," then I was in it! Going into the summer after my eight-grade year, Nicky and I were best of friends. I would see her every time she would come to visit her dad, even talking to her on the phone when she was with her mother. Nicky gave me a sense of happiness, because she did not pass judgment on me. She liked me, for me! As fate would have it, as the summer unfolded, I would find myself living back in Plainfield. I was conflicted at first because I was not sure if I would ever see Nicky again, but I did know one thing, I wanted to move out of my aunt's basement and Edison, NJ.

I would run into Nicky some years later by chance and we caught up on old times; we laughed, we reminisced, and I thanked her for not passing judgment on me during those times. She was beautiful inside and out but at this time she was a young woman blossoming into her own. Nicky would pass away a few years later from an illness, but I still think about her today.

May you always rest in peace, Nicky.

Chapter 7

Welcome to the Hustle

My mother had finally saved up enough money to get her own apartment on the East End. I knew we were moving out of Edison for good, thank God. Lord knows if the eighth grade was any indication of what high school could have potentially been in Edison, the move was right on time! The new apartment was a one-bedroom apartment and I slept on a pull-out couch, which was just fine by me. By that time I'd take anything over a basement.

Looking back, I'm grateful that my aunt let us live in her basement; God knows where I may have ended up at again. Yes, it was not the best place on earth to live, but we made the best of a bad situation. I was curious too why my mother had not moved me in with my father permanently instead of having me live in a basement. Nonetheless, my temporary new home was now on East Front Street in Plainfield, New Jersey.

Although I stayed with my mother briefly at the new apartment, it was only a matter of time before I found myself back at my father's house. It was halfway through the summer when my mom said that I would need to stay with my father for a little while. To me, given my mother's history, I knew that for "a little while" could mean an eternity. Now a full-blown teenager, I was very used to being moved around. In fact, it was more the norm to be on the move than it was to be at one particular place for an extended period. Regardless, I packed my things once again and off to my father's I went.

When I lived in Edison I had no contact with my father or my brothers or sister. While I was living in Edison, my father finally moved into the house on 4th Street that we had been working on previously. Although it was a house, it was still in works to becoming a home. There remained plenty of work to be done, but my father finally got his wish; all of his children were under one roof. I felt a sense of comfort at my father's house. My brothers, sister, and I were tight! I have to admit that at first I felt like an outsider, just a little, but my siblings soon made me forget about those thoughts. My brothers and sister had grown up on the West End, and they had many friends to run the neighborhood with. Naturally, their friends became my friends and those bonds of friendship would last for decades to come, even to this day.

When I stayed with my father primarily, I would find myself staying at my mother's apartment from time to time. Even as a teenager, although I had been through a living nightmare by her hand by then, I still found it in my heart to want to have a relationship with my mother. Time, whether long or short, became paramount for me regarding my mother; I wanted a piece of normalcy with her. Call me a fool, but I could not deny my hunger for some type of motherly affection.

Strangely, I had played football a couple of years as I was whisked away from one living situation to another (as previously mentioned). I was looking forward to playing for the Chiefs on the West End, a local team that was coached by Mr. King, a long-time Plainfield resident, football referee, and mentor to many of the kids in the local neighborhood. We had a decent team, but what was more important was the makeup of the team. Most of the team members either lived on John Street, Essex Street, Third Street or Grant Avenue. From those three blocks, alliances would be formed that would literally become a matter of life or death as a violent and nation-engulfing epidemic was just a year or so away from my freshman year (things would change; call it innocence lost).

During that time, I worked in the Pringles corner store, (now a bodega on the corner of 4th Street and Plainfield Avenue). It allowed me to make my own money and gave me my first taste or responsibility; I was proud. I enjoyed working there as the Pringles became like a second family to me. Ronnie and Reesa Pringle (the store owners) had a younger brother named Fred that I hung out with. Looking back, I'm very grateful to them for giving me my first job.

While working at the Pringle's store, there was a particular girl with a strong southern accent that would come down to the store quite a bit. At first I really didn't pay too much attention to her; there were so many people that would come and go in the corner store. As the "Bricks" (inner city projects) were located right across the street at that time, I did not know too much about them, but I did know that it hosted some of Plainfield's toughest kids. For a mainly East End kid up to that point like myself, I wondered what was I going to do if they came into the store? I dreaded the moment . . . That said, when my little frequent visitor would come into the store it was a welcomed sight!

Fred, who worked with me often at the store said, "Man I think she likes you" (my frequent visitor). Somewhat naïve I said "who, me?" Fred laughed and said "Yes, you!" So the next time the girl came into the store, I decided to tease her some. When she came up to the counter, I asked her what would you like, and she said what sounded like to me, "free-toes" with her southern drawl, and I said we do not sell "free toes" in here. Clearing her throat a little, now a little more confident, she said can I have some free-toes pleeeeeeease, stretching out the please. And I said we do not sell any free-toes heeeeeere, stretching out the word here.

As she fought back her smile, I said "Would you like some Fritos corn chips?" Jokingly, letting out a sigh, she smiled and said yes! I said why didn't you just say that? She said, "I did!" Again jokingly, I said I heard you say "free-toes" not Fritos, who sells free toes? After the ice was broken, I asked her what her name was and she said "Tonya." I said, "nice to meet you, Tonya. Where are you from?" She said Maxton, North Carolina. I said, "Where?" She asked me if I understood English, smiling. Jokingly, I said I did speak English, but I didn't speak Maxton, NC "country talk."

Tonya and I would spend every second with one another from that point on. I gave Tonya my phone number and she called the house, asking to speak to Shaaan. Little Guy, my brother, hung up on her a couple of times saying, "Shaaan doesn't live here." He could not understand what Tonya was saying and really thought the call was for someone else. It was not until I asked Guy "who is that, that keeps calling here?" And he said, "I don't know some country girl that keeps asking for Shaaan." When I finally did speak to Tonya on the phone she said she thought I gave her the wrong number or something. I told her jokingly, "No, my brother could not understand you, like when you say free-toes instead of Fritos" (yes, her southern accent/drawl was that thick).

Although just a few months removed from Nicky, who at that time I still spoke to on the phone, I found myself spending more and more time with Tonya. I asked Tonya how old she was, and she said 13, so I was cool with it. Not knowing she was actually 2 years younger than me, and back then 2 years apart was a lifetime. It would not be until some years later that I would find out that she was actually a few years younger than me.

Tonya's mother lived across the street from my father's house so it was convenient to see her. She actually went to school in the south because her mother wanted her to have a good education without the distractions that city living brought, not that you couldn't get a quality education in Plainfield. That said, in the fall Tonya would go back down south. However, that first summer, Tonya and I were inseparable, literally joined at the hip.

Tonya was a beautiful girl with a southern innocence about her. I found her easy to talk to and we fit together like a hand and glove. Although only 12, by the time that first summer came to an end, she said something striking to me. She looked deeply into my eyes and said "Sean, I'm going to marry you one day!" I said to myself, "yeah right, and I'm Santa Clause!" But, I did know that there was something special about this girl.

The summer drew to a close and I found myself going to stay with my Aunt Evon in Philadelphia for a few weeks. Although we had not talked at all while I was in Philly, because it was a long-distance call for us both, my aunt did allow me to call my father's house from time to time. Not sure if I would get to see Tonya before she left, Tonya came down to my father's house to tell my brother Guy that she was leaving and to please let me know that she was gone the next time he talked to me. The next time I spoke to Guy, he did just that and I knew she would not be there when I returned from Philly.

With the last few weeks of the summer at hand, I had returned to Plainfield, my father's. Tonya was gone and it was football time by then. The Chiefs were gearing up and high school was starting. It seemed like all we did was practice; Mr. King the coach was a perfectionist. Like with any football team something else was catching our eyes, the cheerleaders. Although Tonya had returned south, as the saying goes, "boys will be boys." Even though I was missing my little "country friend," at 14 years of age, I was very easily distracted.

There was one particular cheerleader that I found myself talking to over and over again after practice. It was none other than Danielle, yes, my "sand box" buddy from years back. The one person I had confided so much in as a child, and who I knew I could trust with anything. However, this time we were older, on our way to being freshman and Gerri had developed. What were the chances of her being a cheerleader on my team on the West End of town?

I had lost contact with her up to that point but when we both realized that we were members of the Chiefs football organization we found it incredible. We spent countless hours on the phone playing catch up. She asked me about my mom and I told her that she was fine. She had known Mike had killed himself because she lived in the neighborhood, but she still wanted to know if I was okay regarding it all.

She said that she could not believe that I was gone when my mother had moved me to Florida. She said that she would always look down the street to see if I had come back until Mike killed himself and my mother moved away, even knocking on the door at times asking if I had return from my trip yet. I guess my mother told her I was on a trip, but in actuality I was living in hell on earth. I told her that a lot was going on back then and that my mom did what she thought was the best for me at the time. I apologized for not saying goodbye to her, but she chuckled and said, "You were six, no need to apologize."

I knew I could trust Gerri, so I told her what I had to endure after I moved away when we were kids. I told her that I was dealing with a lot of horrible memories mentally, but that I was maintaining. It was actually nice to open up to a trusted friend; until then I had kept all of the physical and mental abuse bottled up inside. She said that she had thought about me often throughout the years and that she would pray at night for me before she went to bed at times. It was nice to be reunited with Gerri.

With my freshman year of high school starting, it was time to get to the business of being a freshman at Plainfield High School. Because I was out of the loop at Thomas Jefferson Jr. High in Edison, I felt somewhat of a stranger walking in the halls of Plainfield High School. Yes, I had my friends from the block, but in high school it brought in kids from throughout the city.

For school I would find myself laying my clothes out meticulously the night before, making sure that the shirt and pants matched up with the shoelaces. From the money I had earned while working at the Pringle's corner store, I had bought five pairs of Lee Jeans along with 10 LaTiger shirts and five different color Mock Neck shirts. It allowed me to rotate outfits (shirts mainly) without having to buy a lot of pants (an inner city secret). I also had a pair of Spalding white-on-white sneakers that I kept super clean.

In high school I knew one thing—I had to have my dress game on point. If your gear was busted, you got no play with the girls. Given my situation, there was not a lot of money to go around, so I had to make my outfits last. In fact, I would wash my clothes and hang dry them to keep the color from fading; a practice that I still exercise today (old habits are hard to break)!

With my dress game somewhat situated, it was time to concentrate on one thing, simply fitting in. Although I was dealing with a ton of emotional issues, I had to press on with life. I did not want to go through high school socially challenged; Edison, NJ validated that. I had to find that crew or clique that I fit into. Making friends was easy and a lot of those bonds still exist today, but I needed a crew.

Initially, my partners in school (while staying with my father at the start of the school year) were Bob, Terrance (Rappy), Billy-Wray (Jonel), and Kenny (Yalik). Although we did not all necessarily hang together, they were my collective partners. My brother, Darrow, by then a football star, and my sister Lynn were also in the high school just one year ahead of me.

When fall started to take a hold of the season, I was settling in as a freshman. I concentrated on everything except schoolwork. Girls, football, and wilding out (being reckless), were fast becoming the norm of my life. It was the first time I began to say screw it to everything, to live or die really did not matter. At night, I would still wake up out of my sleep as the mental scars were deeply rooted in my subconscious; again I asked, why me? I was beginning to head down that road that has trapped so many troubled youth that share my story. I was beginning to unravel inside; I was clearly on my way to becoming a "statistic."

Halfway through my freshman year, I moved back in with my mother as she was beginning to struggle financially. I took odd jobs to help her offset costs, no longer working at the Pringle's store. At that time I would get out of school and then go to work where I could, even mopping floors at Ferraro's pizza (a local Plainfield eatery) at night. My mother made it clear that the light and food bill would rest squarely on my shoulders. Initially I agreed, but as time would have it, the more I worked and earned, weekends included, the more she would demand and take. She would spend a great number of years chasing lawsuit after lawsuit, and yes I fell into chasing her Holy Grail with her as well. However, I knew I was getting tired of her taking all of my hard-earned money! I didn't mind helping her out, by far, but it was all I had monetarily and my father made it clear that "you would get your own by your own" by then so I could not turn to him.

Now back on the East End of my hometown of Plainfield, I reunited with many of my childhood friends. Many of them had become Five-Percenters. The Five Percent Nation began back in 1964 by Clarence 13X, who was a minister in Mosque no. 7 under the tutelage of Malcolm X. He began teaching that the black man himself was God. Five-Percenters also departed from the Nation of Islam in their teaching of the Supreme Alphabet and Supreme Mathematics, a system devised by Clarence 13X, wherein each letter or numeral denoted a concept with an accompanying parable. "A" stands for Allah, "B" is Be or Born, "C" is see or understanding and so on.

I was instantly drawn to the Five Percent Nation of Islam (5NOI); it gave me, and others like me (inner-city young black males and females), a sense of direction. I immediately set out to become a God or G.O.D. (God Cipher Divine). In school I found an enlightner (a person that could bring me into the 5NOI), M. Holman A.K.A. Master Love and he introduced me to the Five Percent Nation. Master, or "Mas" as he went by, gave me my mathematics, the foundation of the Nation. As with the 5NOI, in receiving my initial set of lessons, I was also to receive my 5NOI attribute (name). Although not a member of the 5NOI, it would be none other than Randy McKinney (of Orange Place and my childhood friend), now known as Bashir or Bash, who would give me the name that would become my signature for decades to come. When I told Bashir that I had become a member of the 5NOI he said, "Sean I have a perfect name for you," True Intelligence God Allah. I said, "True Intelligence God Allah it is . . ."

Now a member of 5NOI, I began to put my one God-given talent to work, my book smarts. The 5NOI lessons became insatiable to me. As I finished the Supreme Mathematics, I moved on to the Supreme Alphabet, the Student Enrollment, the 1-14, Actual and Solar Facts, and any "Plus or Additional Lessons" that I could find. In fact, within months I would have the "120" completely committed to memory, (all the lessons of the 5NOI that were given to me as I progressed through the degrees were committed to memory and understood).

As the 5NOI was being introduced in New Jersey and Plainfield, it was simultaneously taking root throughout New York and Connecticut. The nation was growing and I was a devout student of the lessons. The mastery of the lessons allowed me to exercise the most dangerous part of the body, the mind! I began to enlighten others who wanted to become 5NOI members. Being a part of the 5NOI allowed me to move in certain circles that would otherwise not have been so easily navigated.

Ironically, my grades continued to fall in school; I concentrated my efforts more and more on being a true student of the 5NOI. When it came time for ciphers (a place where 5NOI members gathered and added on to the days "mathematics;" that is, discuss the lessons for the day), I didn't miss a single one. Small in stature, I was very sure of myself when it came to "adding on!" I attended ciphers in the boroughs of New York, as well as North and South Jersey; I was in my comfort zone while "doing the math" as we called it.

Down the street from my mother's apartment was an apartment complex named Town House. Town House was the rival of the Bricks (projects) at the time on the West End, and it housed some of the toughest kids on the East End of town. Within those walls resided plenty of 5NOI members, to whom which I had become close. There was Scientific and his sister Nu Nu, who were like a big brother and little sister to me, Wisdom God Allah; a childhood friend from school, A-Islam, Just Knowledge, B-Divine, Pure, and Shai God to name a few. They called Town House "The Desert" and it would be the first place that I would be exposed to the hustle and what we called "clocking." For the purpose of this book, hustle means drugs, getting high, robbing, stealing, wilding out, and all things that are "perceived" as associated with the "streets."

The Desert also laid claim to Puma Crew, who were guys a little older than us. Many of the members of Puma Crew had younger relatives (cousins or brothers) that were Gods and were members of the Desert. There was never a conflict amongst the two groups that laid claim to Town House. At this time, Hip-Hop was still beginning to sweep across the nation and Town House (as well as Plainfield) laid claim to one of the world's biggest pioneering DJ's of all time, DJ Cheese, who had competed on the world stage (The DMC 1986 World Champion) and without question was amongst the world's elite.

Not realizing it at the time, I had a front row seat as I witnessed the birth of Hip-Hop taking place before me. DJ Cheese made most of the mix tapes in our town (with the exception of a few local rival DJs). There were nights spent in his apartment just watching the birth of Hip Hop unfold as he made one mix tape after another. His DJ equipment was set up in his closet and he never really made a big fuss about who was there to watch him create his mix tapes, as long as you didn't get in the way, and were a member of the "Desert." Of note: Although a historical and cemented figure on the world stage regarding Hip-Hop, he has remained a very humble individual . . . a rare trait these days.

Some decades later, Cheese and I would run into each other at the Boys and Girls Club in Plainfield. We embraced one another and spoke briefly. We would briefly serve on its advisory board together. It was good to see him and that he was doing well in life, and it was even better to see that we both understood that our collective talents would do a greater good towards the youth of our hometown. Although we pursued different avenues in life (Cheese with music and me with my profession), we both ended up at the same door, knocking upon it in hopes of giving back to the youth of our beloved town of Plainfield, New Jersey.

At this time, money was becoming a serious challenge for my mother. Although I was working odd jobs, it just was not enough. The small echo of the hustle was beginning to call me but I fought the temptation for now. It was around this time that my mother and I got some horrible news. Big Jeff, my brother's father in Florida, had been shot and killed. Big Jeff had become a Bounty Hunter some years after I had left Florida, and one of the fugitives that he was trying to apprehend shot and killed him.

Like I stated before, Big Jeff treated me just like I was his own child while I lived in Florida. That said, unlike the Vietnam Veteran Mike, I felt a sense of loss and it touched me to the core. We were unable to attend the funeral because my mother and I didn't have the money or resources to go. We tried to collectively be a support system for my brother little Jeff from a distance. However, I could tell that my mother really took Big Jeff's death hard, as did I.

Big Jeff, with his heart of gold, even in death, found a way to help out my mother. Big Jeff had left his insurance benefits to my mother. Not that it was a lot of money, but it was enough to offset expenses for her and I. She also became the benefactor of his social security benefits as she and Big Jeff never formally ended their marriage. All things taken into account, Big Jeff was a good man and I will forever be in his debt for being there for me when it seemed like I had no one else to turn to at such a tender age. My mother owes him a huge bit of gratitude on many fronts! Big Jeff, may you continue to rest in peace.

Going into the summer of my sophomore year, my grades were horrific! In fact, I had every intention of dropping out of high school as soon as I turned 16. But it was summer and my birthday was months away, so there was trouble to be had and I was game. I continued to float back and forth between my mother and father's house. I also found myself becoming more and more entrenched in the dealings of Town House. The hustle was starting to become more and more an everyday occurrence, and I was slipping more and more into an "I don't care about the world" mentality.

By this time, my crew consisted of Talib, Divine 7, Angelo, C.I. Original, and Al Tariq, all connected to Town House in one way or another. Of note, Me, Divine (John White) and Talib (Todd McClendon) were inseparable. We would practically live in one another's house or apartment one way or another. When it came down to "beefing" (dealing with rivals) we had one another's back; rest assured in Plainfield one way or another, you had beef; it didn't matter how hard you were (win or lose)! Talib was the ladies man and all of the young girls fell in love with his boyish charm. I swear he could charm a snake out of its own skin!

The collective hangout was Fun Time on Route 22, a local highway that ran primarily from Pennsylvania to New York City. My crew hung out there quite a bit as it housed the latest video games and pool tables at the time. It also laid claim to Scotch Plains, NJ crews. Although a fierce rival to Plainfield in sports, it was more serious on the street level. As we were tied up into Town House, it was no mystery that there was no love lost between Town House and anyone who laid claim to Scotch Plains. Oddly, for the most part, the peace was maintained between Plainfield, Town House, and Scotch Plains at Fun Time.

However, one particular time things would take a turn for the worse. As the crew found itself heading back towards Town House, we decided to head down Terrill Road. We were going to stop at an apartment complex close to Fun Time to say what's up to some of our friends that lived in there. At best there were maybe five of us, but the people we were looking for were not there. As we started to make our way back towards the street we noticed a group of guys heading our way, none of them looked familiar! This group fast became a mob and we found ourselves outnumbered seven or eight to one. It was Scotch Plains and they were looking to catch us slipping (caught off guard) on the border of their town. Initially we all agreed to stand and fight, but common sense kicked in and we were forced to get out of there.

As we made our way across the creek, they pursed us, but would only venture so far into Plainfield. Notably about Plainfield, blocks and neighborhoods may fight against one another fiercely, but when it came to "out of towners," you would have thought that we all shared the same biological mother, because we immediately had one another's back (any local dispute amongst each other would be set aside temporarily).

That said, we were still upset at the fact that they had been plotting on us (at Fun Time Skate and Arcade) and following us and getting their numbers right to come after us. Back then, as stated, suede Puma sneakers were in style and of course we were all wearing them at the time. Suffice it to say, water and suede don't mix, so all of our sneakers were destroyed and we all wanted some payback because we were forced to cross a brook in retreat.

Later on that night, we found ourselves at a party on our side of town. Now drunk and full of Old English 800 Malt Liquor, we wanted to wild out at any cost. When the party ended, we came across a rival block member as we headed back towards Town House. We quickly circled around him and asked him what's up. Not afraid, he replied, "What's good?" We replied "you" and began to jump him. When the fight was over we left him sprawled out on the sidewalk. It is the same thing that he and his crew would have done had they caught one of us slipping and on their side of town, so I didn't feel any sense of remorse at the time (it was the law of the land), but looking back, yes, it was wrong.

Knowing that they would be coming after us later that night for retaliation, we all grabbed bats when we made it back to the apartment complex. We all agreed that we were going to handle the situation once it presented itself that night. That said, standing in the front of Talib's mother's apartment, cars passed by with no incident initially. We really thought that just maybe the individual that we had jumped was in no shape to return. Just as we were going to head in for the night, a car slowly made its way down Front Street. Divine (John

White) was the first to spot the vehicle. He said, "Yo something is up with this car, it's moving too slow up the street!" At that time the "drive by" was literally nonexistent so we were not anticipating anything more than a good fistfight.

As the car crept closer and closer, we all got ready, still mad from the Fun Time incident earlier, and plenty left in the tank after jumping the rival block member. Bats in hand, the car finally reached us, someone yelled out, "what's up?" we in-turn yelled back "What's good?" Instead of them getting out of the car to handle the situation with their hands, the back window rolled down slowly as I recall and a bang rang out, coupled with a flash. They were shooting at us, and the situation changed instantly.

The first bullet whizzed past my head missing it by mere inches, it struck the sign that was off to my right. The force of the bullet that struck the sign hit it with such force that it shook the sign back and forth violently. The ringing in my ear was incredible. I hit the ground immediately and everyone thought that I had been shot! Talib and John yelled out my name to see if I was okay, and I said yes (barely able to hear them from the ringing), but the bullets kept coming. We were going to have to make a run for it or die! This time there would be more than just our Puma sneakers getting wet; it could cost us our lives.

When I finally made my way to my feet, I knew I had to move fast. The shooter had now become "shooters" and the shots rang out one after another; me and Talib made our way to the back of the apartment complex and they were in pursuit firing their guns; how no one got shot that night was a pure miracle. We split up in order to make it hard for them to shoot into a group. Talib and me (side-by-side) found ourselves quickly running out of real estate. Once again the same brook that we had visited earlier that evening would again get a visit from Talib and me.

The shooters were what felt like right on our heels, so we made our way to the bank of the brook, placing our backs up against the mud. As the water flowed, it drowned out our heavy breathing, as one of the shooters was right above our head. To this day I thank God that it was pitch black that night and that you really could not see three feet in front of you, because I would have been killed that night. I remember one of the shooters saying right above my head, "Man, where did they go that fast!" They were out for blood that night.

The shooters knew they only had a small window to come after us so they made their way back to the car before the cops came. Eventually we too made our way back to Talib's mother's apartment along with everyone else. Again, by the grace of God no one was shot, but I learned a valuable lesson that night; for every negative action, there would be an equal negative reaction in return, some call it karma. My mother, once I returned to the apartment said, "Sean did you hear all of that gun fire?" I said, "I must have just missed it mom!" I did not want to tell her that it was me that they were after. Unfortunately, it would not be the last time that I would be shot at in my life. To this day, I'm not sure if it was retaliation for the "jumping" or Scotch Plains, but let's just say I'm glad I'm able to share my story. God, always watching over his Bastard Child!

Talib would prematurely lose his life some years later. May he continue to rest in peace; you are missed!

Now in the tenth grade I was still living between my two parents. Living between the two of them provided some type of stability, if I can strangely suggest it. I enjoyed being around my brothers and sisters but I also enjoyed Town House and the 5NOI Gods of the East End. Through it all, up to this point, I continued to place my efforts in all the wrong ways. I didn't take school seriously while still contemplating dropping out of high school. Inside, I was dealing with a ton of demons and I just wanted to end it all. I really didn't care about school. I felt like the beaten Bastard Child and I was reliving the trauma of my childhood up to that point over and over again mentally, still waking up in cold sweats nightly wherever I laid my head. It was even harder to keep up the persona outwardly that I was fine and that nothing was wrong in life.

Mrs. White-James was my high school guidance counselor and the one person who took note of my scholastic potential and the reality of what was going on with my grades. Part way through my sophomore year, she called me into her office for a sit-down to discuss the value of an education. As many others did, I respected Mrs. White-James but I was slowly deteriorating inside and I really did not care much at that point for what she or anyone else had to say. All I knew inside was that I was ready to end it all and that school honestly was the last thing on my mind. Although I did not convey my inner thoughts with Mrs. White-James, what she did next would forever have a profound effect on my life. She said "Sean, I think it would be best if you attended the Scared Straight program . . ." This was the original Scared Straight program of Rahway State Prison, New Jersey that others in the country have since modeled themselves after, to include the television show, *Beyond Scared Straight*.

"Scared Straight, yeah right" I said to myself. I didn't know what it was and I had no plans on going! However, Mrs. White-James (in her ultimate wisdom) did one better; she had already contacted my father and suggested that I attend the program and he agreed. Once I got home to my father's house, he immediately asked me for the permission slip to sign so that I could attend the field trip. There was no way for me to get out of it. Had she not contacted my father, I would have never taken the permission slip home, nor would I have attended the trip. Looking back, I am glad that things unfolded the way that they did.

The day of the trip, I did not know what to expect. The other kids in attendance with me were other kids that the school must have considered at-risk youth. Naturally at that time, there was no Internet; nor was there a Scared Straight television show like there is today to watch before I went. I had no idea what "Scared Straight" entailed or what to expect. While we loaded the bus, Mrs. White-James said "Sean I want you to sit next to me." Why? I thought to myself, but I didn't mind; Mrs. White-James was always a calming figure. While on our way to the program, Mrs. White-James said to me that she could see potential in me and that life at times can be rough, but that life is about choices. In her own way, she was letting me know that I was at that "fork in the road" and she wanted me to see what one of the forks could result in if I took the wrong path.

Once we arrived at the destination, the reality that we were at Rahway, New Jersey State Prison sank in. To a teenager, it was a lot to digest; it was surreal. When we departed the bus, the reality of the moment engulfed me; it was as if no one else was on that bus with me. When we entered the prison we were patted down and cleared to enter. The prison guide gave us a briefing and then showed us the various weapons that the prisoners made out of everyday materials. At that point the program had my undivided attention! We were then escorted into the area where we would be interacting with the prisoners, "lifers!"

I tried to give off the persona that I was not affected by what was going on, but inside I was terrified! The prisoners were escorted by the prison guards coming in, they seemed like giants to me. I was barely 5' 6" and 120 pounds soaking wet. These men were hardcore criminals and made no bones about who they were and why they were there! I found myself enamored by each story that the prisoners presented about themselves.

You could see the sincerity and passion of the moment by each prisoner as they each pleaded to us that "this was not a place that you want to end up at!" The reality of the moment was again sinking in; I knew that this was not a place for me. Many of these men had murdered other human beings, and there was nothing to keep them from doing the same to me if they chose to; after all, as they sternly reminded us, "They were already serving a life sentence." I kept saying to myself, *what if they do kill us?*

Looking back now, I know they were actually helping us but at the time it made for an intense situation. I was getting the message; the more I sat there, the more I knew that prison was not for me. The point was made evident when a prisoner told me to stand up. My knees could barely support me as I was filled with fear, but slowly I made my way to my feet as I tried to play tough. While approaching me he asked me "what size sneaker do you wear?" I gave him the size and he said, "Take off your sneakers" (my coveted Pumas) and that they were his now.

After taking my sneakers, he told me to sit back down and reminded me that if I ever found my way into Rahway State Prison again as an inmate and not a visitor to the program, that I would be his "girl!" At the time, given the size of this man, I remember asking myself how I could stop him if I actually were to find myself locked up in Rahway State Prison. I would not get my sneakers back until we left the program. I could see Mrs. White-James plan unfolding and I would keep the trip to the prison forever engrained into my mind as I approached situations that could put me in prison. They wanted us to learn from their mistakes and it was their way of trying to make a difference from behind bars.

Heading back to the high school, with my sneakers now back on my feet, I again found myself sitting next to Mrs. White-James. Her message was simple, "Sean, change your ways before it is too late."

I am forever in debt to Mrs. White-James for what she did for me, as well as the prisoners of the original Scared Straight Program of Rahway, New Jersey. I credit them and the program with being my very first point of consciousness regarding the hustle, the streets, and its consequences. The program also forced me to reexamine my position regarding dropping out of high school at 16; I would decide to stay in school.

To the Scared Straight program and the inmates of Rahway State Prison of New Jersey who supported it, thank you!

Chapter 8

The Wild, Wild West

Now going into my junior year of high school, there was an invasion that engulfed the tri-state area like locust—crack cocaine was making the "have-nots," have! Blocks were clearly becoming defined as money and territory became staples of the city. On the "West End" of Plainfield, you had West Third Street, The Hill, Stebbins and 3rd, Halsey (The Honchos from 3rd), the Bricks, the New Projects, Monroe Ave, Arlington Ave and Evona Ave, and my block John Street, better known as the JSP or the Sex Street Posse. On the East End of town, you had Town House (as previously mentioned), 5th Ave, and Meadow Brook Village.

The money was fast and plentiful but as with all things in the hustle, it presented a new set of rules, we began to "play for keeps." *Scarface* served as our 70's version of The Mac and Cleopatra Jones; we must have watched that movie a hundred times as we recklessly ran the "streets" of the Wild West End. We began to turn into new age hustlers; gunplay began to slowly work its way into territorial beefs. Although a good fistfight was still the first choice at that time, gunplay could not be dismissed! My first gun was a Cobalt black .25 Caliber Pistol, and sadly to say now, I knew I could kill if I had to as my street baptism continued in the game. As the saying goes, "it's hard growing up in the ghetto!" Not that I was any tougher than the next kid, but at some point in the hustle you were guaranteed to have beef (a problem with someone), it was the nature of the beast.

It was a time when you could go to Dapper Dan's and purchase a handmade MCM, Polo, or Louis Vuitton suit, drop a thousand dollars on it, and not even think twice about it. The many trips to Broad Street in Newark, NJ gave us access to the big gold ropes of the day; and in Harlem, NY you could find the latest Puma and Adidas sneakers at VIM that no one had on the block, yes it made for a plentiful time amongst hustlers.

During this time, I still struggled even more with school. Although I had money from the streets, I found myself at odds with my conscience—that inner voice that reminded me of the Scared Straight visit would tap me on the shoulder from time-to-time and put things into perspective for me. However, no one was hiring a young black male from the West End of Plainfield at the time and meals and clothing fell squarely on me. I found myself diving deeper into the hustle and deeply committed to the streets, John Street, the "JSP" to be precise, and everything that went with it. After all, it's JSP4L (John Street Posse 4 Life). Once a posse member, always a posse member, 'til death (One way or another as the saying went) . . .

My home life was starting to feel the effects of the invading crack epidemic as I stayed permanently with my father at this point, but again anything to do with my wellbeing was on me; I had no help! Slowly but surely the hustle would put its vice grips on the place I called home. School was more and more a distant memory while I tried to keep my head above water with my grades, but having to take care of myself found me visiting Maslow's Hierarchy of needs. The clothes I wore, the shoes on my feet, were all bought by way of the hustle. With my back against the wall, I had no place to go and nowhere to turn literally. John Street fast became my family; the same guys that I played football with for Mr. King were now my partners in crime! It was clearly a time of innocence lost. Trips to New York to re-up on the hustle made for day trips during school. I would even find myself taking a borrowed car to New York to re-up; it was nothing for a "crack head" (a person addicted to Crack Cocaine) to loan you their car (whether you had a license or not back then).

At that time, I thought the only way to make a dollar was by way of the streets (yes, looking back I know better now). Because of the high crime rate associated with the drug game, and the apparent face attached to it (mainly young black males at the time) it made for an impossible hill to climb to land a job. I applied to what seemed to be every store in Plainfield and the surrounding area, but no one wanted to hire a rough-around-the-edges young black male from the West End of Plainfield, New Jersey. I felt like my back was against the wall when it came to surviving on my own; I was a teenager, barely past 10th grade and odd jobs were not going to cut it.

The hustle got more serious as time progressed; it became my only source of income. Close calls with the law put my future (whatever it may have been at the time) in jeopardy foolishly. As the saying goes again, "God looks after fools and babies!" Well, I was no infant, so God clearly was protecting a young fool involved in a dangerous game called the hustle. The money poured into John Street non-stop, day and night, seven days a week; it had become the great equalizer of cash for those who did not have, versus those who had. Luck would serve on my side on many occasions, even when my life was at stake in the hustle.

Trips to my house on West 4th Street to "re-up" on the hustle was an everyday ritual; it was a walk up the street, one right turn, and eight houses down (now a vacant lot), and there sat my home. I must have taken that trip dozens if not a hundred times. Luck on my side (again God watching over a fool), the cops, or Five-O as we called them back then, never caught me transporting the hustle back to the block. However, karma was working its way towards me; it was only a matter of time before the streets would come and ask for my soul again.

I had become a creature of habit in the game (which goes against all the rules of hustling). I had no idea that I was being watched by an individual that had planned to rob and kill me. He had to have watched my daily routine, as he calculated his next move. This particular day, as with any other day, after I was done on the block, I headed home to re-up on the hustle. The robber (or "stick up kid" as we called them back then) was going to make his move on me this day, little did I know. He had to have watched my movements for weeks prior to his attempt. I never traveled to the house with anyone, and I always went to the block on my own when I was "dirty" (in possession of the hustle). The stick up kid knew this as he watched my movements methodically I'm sure.

While I was returning to the block, something didn't feel right; call it intuition (my gut)! Normally I walked on the sidewalk so that I could stay as close to the houses just in case the cops came; that way I could run between the houses and go into the graveyard that ran parallel with John Street to get away. However, on this day, something told me to walk in the street when I turned the corner.

The abandoned house on the corner of 4th and John Street in Plainfield (formerly Big Sis's corner store) had a small vacant lot behind it. This is where the stick up kid was going to make his move. He planned to catch me walking past the abandon house, rob me, kill me (fearing getting caught or retaliation if he left me alive) and dumping my body in the bushes of the vacant lot.

With my sock full of the hustle, and by chance a 40 Ounce of Old English Malt liquor in hand, I made my way around the corner. As I walked past the fire hydrant on the corner of 4th and John Street, instead of staying to the left of the hydrant (the side walk) I chose to swing out into the street as I previously mentioned (that gut feeling was talking to me). The stick up kid was in position and waiting, as the bulk of the John Street Posse hung out on the midpoint of the street (where John Street and Essex Street joined), he had to feel that the odds were in his favor. I know he had to be anticipating my route, having watched my movements for weeks I'm sure, but I deviated. As I turned the corner, I'm sure he saw me move between the houses on 4th street.

Only by the grace of God, I moved further into the middle of the street, it was dark with only the street lights providing some type of visibility (lucky, because it was the norm to shoot out the street lights in order to keep the block dark for hustling); he sprang out from behind the abandoned house; however, he had miscalculated my movements.

The sound of the bushes grabbed my attention, startled, I immediately looked to my left, and there he stood with about 20 feet between us, he knew that his robbery had not gone as planned because I was not where he anticipated me to be. I could see the long knife in his hand as we stared each other down. My heart was pounding; he was "playing for keeps," and like a lion or tiger that missed a kill; the hunt and determination was still burning inside of him. As he came towards me he raised the knife; armed with just a 40 Oz bottle of Old English or "Old Gold" as we called it back then, I had one chance to defend myself and save my life.

What seemed like slow motion at the time actually happened very fast. I took the 40-ounce bottle in hand and threw it at his head and face as hard as I humanly could, knowing that if I missed, I was dead! As the half empty bottle shattered, he stumbled forward, determined still; blood was streaming from his head and face, he dropped the knife, but tried to grab me while holding his other hand on his face to wipe the blood. I could tell that he was hurt bad; luckily I was able to get away from him.

I ran down the block and told them that someone had just tried to rob me (which during the height of the crack epidemic was very common). When we walked up the block, the robber had apparently made his way to his feet and disappeared through the graveyard, a place where you didn't want to go at night. I looked for the knife but could not find it, so I assumed that the stick up kid found it and took off. Karma had taken a hold of me again. I was doing wrong and what one puts out in life, karma brings back, yes even if it meant your life; I took it as a warning from God, a close call that could have ended my life early, I was still a teenager! However, I still had to eat and put clothes on my back, so foolishly I charged it "to the game!" The hustle continued for me . . .

To note, "Stick up kids" were an everyday part of life in the hustle. At some point in the hustle, you would be confronted by this harsh reality. Most stick up kids played for keeps (were willing to take your life if need be).

While the school year progressed, I did the bare minimum to get by. The hustle had afforded me the clothes that I wanted and the sneakers of the day. However, more and more that little voice called [reason] continued to grow within me. The months passed by, school parties, the Perth Amboy, NJ Cinema, New York, NY, all became like home. To get a quality fake ID was nothing in New York City. A couple of hundred dollars and you had what looked like a valid ID card for college that would get you into any club or nightspot. The Zan Zabar club or the "ZANZZ" in Newark, NJ was the spot to get your house music groove on, and after the night ended (which was actually the dawn), the love motels made for a great crashing spot.

Club Sensations in Elizabeth, NJ was another place to get your chill on. The John Street Posse would hang out all night in these spots; yes the world was our oyster. The cars were easy to come by, the "3 Series BMW" and Jetta's chromed out were unmistakable. Sometimes between the three allied blocks, John Street, Grant and 3rd (football friends from years past Jeffrey H. and Darryl AKA heavy), and the Honchos From 3rd (C-Born, Foldge, Beeb, Skinner, Tiheem and my cousin Howie or Haleem to name a few) there would be a line of "Bonneville 98 cars" that stretched all the way down the block when we headed out to wherever the night took us. We were always "deep" (had our numbers up) heading out of town—there's safety in numbers. However, the hustler's mask that I was wearing was glued to my face by fast money, girls, and good times! But underneath that mask resided a young black male who was really at odds with his psyche who struggled with the right and wrong decisions of the day.

Most nights after running the streets, I would go back to my room in the attic. My bed consisted of a series of milk crates placed side-by-side, three across with five rows in length in a wooden frame, slim mattress with a blanket on top. You would think that with all the money being made I would have bought a new bed (I could not fit a bed along with my brother in the small space). The attic was hot and cramped in the summer and cold in the winter, but it was home. I had a place to lay my head at a minimum, but the roaches were everywhere. Making sure that no roaches were in my bed before going to sleep was an everyday ritual!

At this point, meals were even coming by way of the hustle. I could easily purchase a hundred dollars worth of food stamps for twenty-five dollars cash. At the time, it seemed all too easy to do, but looking back, it was the absolute wrong thing to do. Those food stamps were a family's only way of eating, who was I to selfishly take advantage of this? If I could go back in time, I would do so many things different. My mind at that time was in such a tailspin, I needed comfort, understanding, I was falling apart at the seams inside, disgusted by who I had become.

Going into my senior year that summer (only by the grace of God), I found myself becoming more and more of a monster; the streets were taking a toll on me. I needed an outside influence to reel me back into reality. Tonya, my southern friend (Ms. "Fritos"), was back in town from North Carolina. She was just what the doctor ordered. Everyone knew me as "True" now, but she refused to call me that, sticking to her guns and calling me Sean. She said "I met you as Sean, and that's what I'm going to call you." Strangely I didn't argue the point; she brought a sense of reason to my life. I could just be "Sean" with her, no cool guy image needed. I would find myself hustling just enough to meet my living needs and then spending as much time with her as possible. I was falling in love as a man, not a boy, for the very first time in my life.

That same summer, the house that I lived in slowly began to succumb to the crack epidemic that was claiming so many victims. The house no longer had running water or electricity; I had no place to turn. I found myself spending as much time with Tonya as possible. Her mother would cook dinner and I would find myself eating at her home daily, passing along the Food Stamps that I would buy on the street. In order to have lighting in my home, we would use kerosene lanterns. By chance, we had acquired a "water key." The key would allow us to turn the water on briefly and take care of our daily needs, until the water company came and put an end to it. I could not invite anyone into the place I was living because of the living conditions. However, it was home, and I had to make the best of a deteriorating situation.

That same summer, Tonya would find herself getting into a serious confrontation with some local girls from the neighborhood. Still unclear to this day why it happened, a fight broke out between Tonya and the girls. By all accounts, Tonya held her own during the fight, not backing down to the girls.

When I asked Tonya what happened, she said that she and the girls had been going back and forth with each other and that it was only a matter of time before it would come to a head! My first concern was making sure she was not injured. As a result of the fight, Tonya's mother pressed charges against the girls. It would mean that Tonya, who normally returned to Maxton, North Carolina for the school year, would have to come back to New Jersey once the court date was set.

With the summer coming to a close, I found myself once again contemplating school my senior year. I knew school would be a struggle because everything was squarely on my shoulders at this point. As the months got colder, living in the house on 4th street became more and more impossible. The heat in the house was provided by kerosene heaters and just about every meal was fast food. Now that Tonya was back down south and I no longer ate meals at her mothers' home, I found myself staying in hotels for weeks on end or until I felt completely paranoid in a given hotel room (afraid that the police would kick in the door at some point). I even tried living with my mother again but it was not meant to be; she was dealing with her own demons.

Chapter 9

Dancing With the Devil

Life was at a standstill for me and I had no one really to turn to. I had been through so much up to that point; I had buried so much pain beneath the mask I was wearing. I didn't know who to turn to at the time; I couldn't let the world know how I was really feeling inside. Foolishly I kept thinking, "What would everyone think of me?" I felt like I didn't have anyone I could really talk to about my most inner thoughts, which would have been a sign of weakness.

Right around December of 1985, Tonya returned to Plainfield to go to court regarding the altercation earlier that summer. I was so happy to see her! As soon as she got in town, she made her way to me. It was just what the doctor ordered! Briefly, I was able to escape what was going on inside of me. For the few days she was in town, I actually got to get away from John Street and we spent all of our time together. We even found ourselves alone at her mother's house.

My baptism in the streets regarding the hustle and women had exposed me to many guilty pleasures way before my time. I found myself wanting Tonya to give herself knowingly to me, and hesitantly she welcomed my advances; we would consummate the relationship that night. In the few days we had before she returned down south, we laughed and joked about being able to see one another again without it being summer time. When the inevitable time came for her to leave, she said goodbye to go back down south, I knew she was pure at heart and that if not me, she would make some man a good wife.

Tonya was gone and now I had to turn my attention back to the everyday grind of the savage streets that greeted me day-to-day. I toiled with school; my grades were a joke at this point. To be honest, I felt that I didn't need school, nor did I have anyone to push me my senior year to graduate. My role models were hustlers. I was fast on my way to becoming another statistic—a young black male without a high school diploma destined for the grave yard or jail. Who was to blame? I had been through so much that I really didn't care about life anymore.

My routine still consisted of waking up, cutting school, hitting the block, or going to New York first to "re-up" on the hustle, and then "hitting the block." I continued this routine for a few months after Tonya had departed. Ignorance was bliss and I really thought that I could get by in life by continuing to do what I did, hustle!

Although I knew it was wrong, the game, the glitz, and the glamour that came with the hustle and the streets had me lassoed. I was dancing with the devil daily. Add to that, many of my friends at the time that were also lassoed were getting locked up behind the hustle game, but I always thought, "Not me!" On the surface, it looked like people were getting locked up just to be back on the streets some months later. But, in actuality it was the "365 plea bargain" that many of my friends were taking. As crime rose with the crack epidemic, there was a cry from the general public for law enforcement to hammer down on the crack invasion; they wanted metrics, hard numbers showing conviction rates of crack/drug dealers. As a result, many drug dealers took the "365 plea bargain" which gave the general populous the conviction rates that they called for. It would take me years later to realize what actually was happening to our young black males.

Yes, the drug dealer would be back on the streets in a matter of months, but what they didn't realize at the time was that they were actually putting a felony drug conviction on their record that would follow them for the rest of their lives, keeping them out of the military service, civic jobs, etc . . . little did they or I know. Many of my friends during that time took the plea bargain, ignorant of the ramifications it would have on them in the years to follow. Many should have fought their cases; some were clearly innocent, some guilty as charged, some got caught with someone else's "stash" (drugs) or in the proximity of one, but were afraid to fight it in court for fear of a lengthy jail sentence. Had I been caught, I too would have taken the "365" Plea Bargain. God was truly looking out for me as I foolishly danced with the devil daily.

Around February of my senior year, Tonya's cousin told me that Tonya needed to speak with me. Excited, and not having spoken with her since her December visit, I found my way to a phone. The conversation started off with some small talk and then Tonya said that she had something to tell me. My heart sank, thinking that her mother was not going to let her come back up north for the summer to visit. I said "Tonya, what is it?" She said Sean I'm pregnant! I sat silent on the phone momentarily. She said "hello!" I said, "I'm here . . ." I then asked the obvious but absolutely wrong question, "Am I the father?" She said yes! Life from that moment on would change for me. Here I am barely holding it together, a mental wreck, and now I'm going to be a father.

I was 17 and Tonya was 15—too young to be parents—and I was in no position to be a father. I felt an immense sense of guilt for putting Tonya in this position, although as the saying goes, "it takes two to Tango!" It was my advances on Tonya (a result of my fast living) that ultimately put us here; I selfishly pursued the moment. Tonya being younger and somewhat naïve from the south, it was my responsibility to protect that intimate moment where her innocence were lost.

During the phone conversation, we both knew that we were going to keep the child, an alternative was never up for discussion. I knew it would be hard for Tonya because she was so young—15 and in the Deep South. I told her I would be there for her no matter what. Tonya was a tough girl and I prayed that she could handle it. In fact, truth be told I think she did a lot better than I did. I didn't let anyone know of her pregnancy while she was living down south. I spoke with her mom frequently and assured her that I would be by her daughter's side.

Right around March or April of my senior year, I knew I was not going to graduate. I had finally become that statistic, a young black male, uneducated with no hopes of a future, caught waist-deep in the streets and with a child on the way. I could not believe what was happening. I wanted to do all the right things, but all of the wrongs things were happening!

May of that year, Tonya finally returned to Plainfield because the schools down south went into summer recess before the northern schools. Her stomach had a little poke to it and there was no doubt that in a few months I would be a father. Tonya and I became inseparable and I would spend as much time at her mother's house as she would allow. The house that I stayed in had become a full time residence for the hustle. The last thing I needed Tonya to do was to get caught up in a raid that would find her locked up and pregnant. Besides, it was a dangerous place for anyone, as all walks of life found their way to the house for the hustle.

School was no longer a priority for me; I had failed in high school. Besides, who needed a high school education, right? I was doing just fine by way of the hustle I thought. I had no intentions of ever going back to school—good riddance! As the summer months passed by and my child was soon to be born, Tonya at such a young age, 16, said, "Sean, you have to go back to school. If not for me, for our child!" Again I thought *yeah right* at the embarrassment of going back to school; after all, I didn't do so great the first 4 years. Not that school was a challenge, again, I was a closet bookworm, but life had a vice grip on me and hey, I was doing everything on my own by this point!

Tonya's words began to reverberate in my mind; I knew ultimately she was right. I knew that I had to get it together. I didn't want my child to have to be born to a father who had just given up on life at such a young age. How could I look my child in the face in the years to come and tell that child to pursue her dreams, or get an education when I failed to do so myself? I needed to get it together; I needed to realize that there was a bigger picture. The message was getting through to my thick head, slowly but surely.

The bigger Tonya's belly got, the more my conscience made me realize that school was a must. I told Tonya that if I went back to school that I would need her support; I would need her to wake me up in the mornings and to do my homework at her house because of the living conditions at the house I was staying in—abandon and no lights! As young as we were, the stakes were high but she had my back.

September of 1986, my first daughter Tyneshia Tyshea Hoggs was born into this world; I was a proud father at the ripe old age of 18. Tyneshia was a combination of our two names (Tonya and Sean). The moment she was born, I knew I had to get it together, not by words, but by action. A few days later I would find myself walking back into Plainfield high school after my class had graduated earlier that June, it was a very humbling experience. I fixed my mind on graduating! Dinner, homework, and time with my daughter became my daily routine at Tonya's and then it was off to the streets.

Still looking for some type of direction in my life besides "knowing that I needed to graduate," I found myself in one of the most unlikely of classes, Air Force Jr. ROTC. My guidance counselor thought that I could use the structure, not that it was a place to put "at-risk youth," but that it would instill some type of discipline in me. Reluctant, I agreed to the class. Lieutenant Colonel (Ret.) Rubel was the Senior Aerospace Instructor for the class. He drove a red Porsche 944 and I thought to myself, *he's done something right in life to be driving that.* He immediately made me a "Flight Sergeant" in the class, responsibility that I did not want initially! He said that I was older and that maybe some of the younger students would listen to me; I thought, whatever!

Because the program was new to the high school, in its second year, getting issued my uniform took a bit of time. However, once I received my uniform and wore it in public, I noticed something immediately—people began to speak to me that normally turned their noses up at me or looked at me as a mere street thug. I began to respect the uniform after initially hating it. I actually took my duties in the classroom very seriously.

For the first time in my life I felt like I could stick my chest out and be proud. Oddly enough, it helped me emotionally as it became a bright spot in my life outside of my daughter and Tonya. Lieutenant Colonel Rubel would spend so much time working with me, I just could not understand why. Maybe he saw something in me that I did not see in myself. Although Jr. ROTC was the bright spot of my second senior year in high school, after school each day I was dealing with being a young father, the hustle, taking care of myself, and wondering if this world was ever going to deal me a fair shake on anything. I know now that life is not fair, but back then I asked myself the question.

As the school year progressed, Tonya and I became like a hand in glove, where you would see her you would see me and vice versa. I found myself spoiling my daughter with whatever I could afford, even foolishly showering her with hundred dollar bills at times from the hustle. The one thing that I didn't want to do is to get locked up; that would have left Tonya alone with my daughter (although her mother was there for her). I wanted to be a father, I wanted to be in her life from the beginning; I didn't want her to have to experience what I had to experience years earlier regarding my parents. I made my mind up and said that I would do everything in my power humanly to find a legitimate job. Again after having so many doors slammed in my face regarding a job, I knew I was in for an uphill battle, or so I thought.

Jimmy M. lived up the street from me had worked his way up to manager at Wendy's Hamburger's. I made it my business to go up to Wendy's and apply for a job, hoping that when Jimmy reviewed my application, I would be in. I had to put down Tonya's mother number to be reached. Of course I "greased the skids" and told Jimmy that I was looking to work at Wendy's and looking for a little help in getting employed. Jimmy made me promise him not to "blow it" if he hooked me up with a job. I swore to him that I would show up on time and work my butt off if he gave me a job.

Jimmy was a man of his word and I was a man of mine, knowing that I wanted to change my life for the better, I made it a point not to let Jimmy down. I finally had a job and I would find myself working like a dog to make ends meet. I did not care how many hours I had to work; I wanted to make an honest living. From the checks I received, I would always make sure that Tonya had money in her pocket for our daughter's needs. What was left over from my check would go to my everyday living expenses. The money I was bringing in were mere crumbs, but I was proud of every cent that I earned honestly.

As the school year progressed, I knew I was actually going to graduate. Although laying my head in a comfortable place was still an everyday struggle, I knew I had done enough in high school to finally graduate. I began to think about an even bigger prize—college. Who would have thought that it would have been an option for me? I applied to a few local schools with hopes of maybe attending college. I was initially afraid to apply to college because of my academic record that returned me to high school for a second senior year. I turned to Lieutenant Colonel Rubel for some guidance and he told me that I owed it to myself to at least try, so "try" I did.

Of all the schools that I applied to (praying that I got into Rutgers University, the state school of New Jersey), only one college opened their doors for me to a degree; Rutgers was the first school to say no, and rightfully so. Kean College of New Jersey had sent a letter to Tonya's mother's house (now my mailing address) and the letter requested my presence at the campus for an interview regarding admission into the Exceptional Educational Opportunity (EEO) program. The EEO program was a program designed to assists students who did not meet general admission criteria, but had the potential to succeed in college.

Excited, the day came for the interview. I nervously sat in the admissions hall waiting for my name to be called; I had on a pair of Jeans, Timberland boots, and a "hoodie" (not knowing any better). There were so many other kids there nicely dressed; I thought I had no chance at getting into the school. Finally, the time came and my name was called. My heart pounded as I slowly rose to my feet. I walked towards the door where they called my name; Mr. Jeremiah Dix greeted me. He extended his hand and I shook it then he told me to have a seat. He had all of my high school transcripts right there in from of him; it was not a pretty sight.

He told me that it would be hard for me to get accepted into the program based on my academic record. Not that I had a transcript riddled with "F's" only, it was that I was inconsistent with my approach to school. One semester would be great and the next would be all "F's." I had the SAT scores to get accepted into the school (nothing spectacular) but I did not have the academic continuity that they were looking for. I felt that my pursuit of college was becoming nothing more than a mere pipe dream.

Mr. Dix asked me "if I give you a chance and I let you into this program, will you succeed?" I replied, "Yes!" I pleaded my case to him, and shared my situation up to that point with him and said, "All I need is a chance." He said that he could not make any promises but that he understood my situation. I made a promise to him that if he let me into the program, I would finish my degree.

A few weeks later, a letter came to Tonya's house; it was from Kean College. I didn't open the letter immediately because I didn't want to face another let-down in life. In fact, I let the letter sit for a few days before I got up enough nerve to open it up. Tonya by my side in her living room with my daughter between us, I finally opened the letter. It said, "Congratulations on being accepted into the EEO program of Kean College of New Jersey." I sat there initially, in disbelief that I was accepted into the program. Mr. Dix had found a way to let me into the program; I felt an immense sense of gratitude towards him.

Now at senior night at Plainfield high school, the school was honoring those students who were accepted into college and who were receiving school honors. When they asked all of the students who have been accepted into college to rise, I stood up slowly, many were shocked to see me stand up (I think because this was my second go round as a senior in high school and I was no poster child), but it was a proud moment for me regardless. I felt like a million dollars in that brief moment and I knew that it could never be taken away from me.

In the weeks to come, I got ready to graduate from high school. I could not believe that it was all coming to an end. Times were still tough, but at least I knew at a minimum that I would have a high school diploma to arm myself with as I faced an unknown future (in large part to Tonya, who was two years my junior).

Graduation day was finally at hand; Tonya was there along with my daughter. I had my robe, hat, and tassel, and I was really getting ready to walk across the stage as a high school graduate. Many members of the John Street Posse and 5NOI were in attendance to support me; one of their own was getting "that piece of paper" that had eluded so many of us. It was not easy, but I had done what seemed to be the impossible. When my name was called and I finally received my diploma in hand, I felt like someone for the very first time in my life. I had fought through so much just to get to this point that it all seemed surreal. However, I had one more order of business that day.

When the crowd thinned out at the end of the ceremony, instead of heading home, I walked back up to the high school alone. I told Tonya that I would meet her back at her house. Once there, I sat on the bench right outside of the entrance to the school. I didn't sit there for a few minutes, I sat there for an hour or so reflecting on all of the hard work and incredible odds I had to overcome just to get to that point; I was overcome with emotion.

Before starting college that Fall, two things had to happen: one, I had to successfully complete the Kean College EEO summer program, and two, I had to stop working at Wendy's because I had to reside on campus that summer—a stipulation of the EEO program. I thanked Jimmy for giving me the opportunity to work at Wendy's and off to the Kean College EEO summer program I went.

When I got to college that first day, they had us all sit in a large room. We were given the goals and objectives of the EEO program. Eerily Mr. Dix, now center stage, addressed the summer EEO class in its entirety. He told us to "look to the left of one another and then look to the right of one another." He said that half of us would not be in the program by the end of our projected senior year. I sat there confident and said, "I'll be here!"

Throughout the summer, Tonya would come up to my dorm with my daughter; she would cook for my roommates and me and it brought a sense of comfort. I tried my best to do the right thing while I was in college. Something I did not anticipate were the parties that took place in college. Unlike high school, you had students from all over the state and beyond that were there for the summer program. As the summer progressed, I became more interested in hanging out, then schoolwork. It was a new environment for me, one where everyone for the most part got along. I was fast becoming friends with people and college seemed like a good fit for me, almost too good!

During this time, I became close with my Resident Assistant (RA), Chris. Chris was a member of Omega Psi Phi Fraternity, and we clicked instantly. He became my first positive role model in my life. I remember he would be working on papers for school while doing his job as the RA, in addition to being very active in his fraternity. He was all about positivity and he was my first point of consciousness regarding strong black role models; remember, up to that time my role models were all from the streets.

Chris would take me over the summer to various business meetings that he was involved in. In fact, he was the one who actually took me out to buy new clothes, as he wanted to introduce me to a positive environment. He told me that Timberland Boots, baggy pants, and loose-fitting shirts weren't the answer (standard gear for me up to that point and all I knew). From his own pocket, he bought me a few pair of dress pants, some shirts, and ties. He told me that he saw something in me that I did not see for myself and that I needed to carry myself beyond the streets. He said, "Sean, you have a gift and you need to use your talents for the right things in life." I could tell the sincerity in his words and he struck me as a person who commanded respect. Circle after circle, he would let me and a few other students tag along with him in them.

Although I enjoyed college and being exposed to so many different things that were positive, the fact remained that I was failing out of the program. Between being a father, school, and the streets, I was burning my rope at both ends. Something had to give! With the summer program coming to a close, sadly I knew I was on my way out. I felt like I let the world down, moreover, I felt like I let Mr. Dix down the most. There I was with an opportunity that could have gone to a more deserving student that would have finished the program and I blew it.

I didn't have the nerve to face Mr. Dix, Chris, or any of the friends that I had made. It was impossible for me to juggle it all at the same time. When the fall semester came to pass, I became nothing more than another college dropout. College as I knew it would become nothing more than a distant memory. I would never return to the campus of Kean College as a student again.

Chapter 10

The Man in the Mirror

Now back at home on the block, I returned to the ways I was all too familiar with. The image that I was now seeing in the mirror had my face and my body, but my soul had turned into something I simply did not recognize anymore. I could not return to Wendy's because that was a bridge that was burnt when I moved on to college. I continued to look for a job, ultimately landing one at White Castle's Hamburgers. Tonya also had a part-time job at Pizza Hut as we pulled our money together to make ends meet as a couple. Tonya still had a year left in high school so any plans for the future with her would be put on hold for now. I held the White Castle job for a while until I was eventually fired. Transportation had become an issue and I just did not have a way or means to get to work. I could only bum but so many rides to work before it became a burden to those that I asked. With my back to the wall again I turned to the hustle to make ends meet. Anything that I could get my hands on, any odd job, I would take it.

Graduation approached for Tonya and I began to contemplate asking her to marry me. The one definitive thing that I did know is that she was the one person in the world who made me happy. Although we were kids, or young adults for that matter, we were a strong couple, more than mere "high school sweethearts." Strangely her words of marrying me when she was just twelve years of age were coming to pass.

Spring had arrived and I found myself running out of options. The house that I lived in was now a full-blown crack house. I had nowhere else to turn; it was my home and I had to make the best of a crazy situation. If I was not on the block, I would be at Tonya's house with her and my daughter. It even got to be the case that wherever I laid my head, that would be my home for the night, at times even sleeping outside on a porch or in a car. However, the more I ran the streets, the more I realized that I needed to get off of them. It was only a matter of time before I would find myself dead or in jail behind the streets. The Scared Straight visit remained that tiny little voice in my head that tempered my actions still. Trips to New York City became very dangerous, as the places that I frequented would greet me with high caliber weapons and powerful handguns when "business" was conducted. I was playing foolishly with my life in a game that had no margin for error at this point.

Now June, Tonya was finally going to graduate. I had made my mind up and I had decided to ask Tonya, just a month removed from her 18th birthday, to marry me. I had purchased a ring (trust me, nothing fancy), and I knew when and where I was going to "pop the big question."

Prior to asking for her hand in marriage, I did ask her mother and father if I could have their permission to marry their daughter. Her mother, initially hesitant, asked me what were my plans and how would I take care of her daughter and granddaughter? I had no real answers! I just knew that I wanted to marry her daughter more than anything in the world. She said that I could have her blessing if I had a solid plan for the future regarding her daughter and granddaughter.

I knew once her mom agreed that her father would also agree, which he did. I told Tonya's mother that we would not get married until I was able to put a roof over her daughter's head and clothes on her and my daughter's back. That said, her mother knew that my situation was a tough one so at best it would be some time, if not years before we would get married.

The day of her graduation I finally popped the big question! Tonya almost tackled me with her hug as she said "Yes!" Tonya was the one person in the world that I knew without question believed in me, even when I did not believe in myself. Immediately I knew I had to get it together. Tim, who was a member of the JSP, worked at AT&T and said that he would be able to get me a job in the mailroom. He told me that I would need dress pants, a shirt, and a tie. I said, "Not a problem," I still had the clothes that Chris from Kean College had bought me. For the next few months, I found myself working in the mailroom. My aunt Cynthia even let me move in with her for a while and sleep on the couch, not charging me much for rent.

Tonya would pick me up and drop me off to work each day. This lasted for weeks but eventually the job fell apart because transportation had again become an issue (like with White Castle restaurant). Tonya's mother had switched shifts on her job and Tonya could no longer pick me up or take me to work.

Worth noting, at this time my license was suspended and I had a nice surcharge from the state for not paying any of my previous tickets that I had acquired, so buying my own car was out of the question, since they would run my license. Tonya's mother would not let me put a car in her daughter's name either, which I couldn't blame her for.

Once again I found myself on the "street corner" of John and Essex Street; I just could not catch a break. When it rained it poured . . . However, I would get a wakeup call from life by way of the streets, moreover by a man named Danny, or "Danny Do-Whop" as we called him, that would forever cement my direction in life.

Danny was a dope fiend and would hustle dope all night. His hands were as big as boxer mitts, swollen from injecting heroin into them over the years. Danny had to be in his 50's and was a carryover from the hustle days of the 70's. He could move about the various blocks with impunity and could hustle dope like no other. I kept saying to myself, with the energy that this man put into hustling and banging (injecting dope into his veins), there is no telling what he might have become in life if he put his efforts into something constructive. I was asking myself, would this be me in the years to come? I knew I wanted better . . .

I watched Danny prepare a bag of heroin after a night of hustling. He was methodical laying out everything he needed. His arms were so skinny. I remember he took off his belt and wrapped it around his arm. He put the excess belt in his teeth to keep the slack tight. He had heated the heroin in a spoon, it was now liquid, and I sat there thinking to myself, how many times has he done this? He stuck the needle in his arm slowly after finding a vein, sweat beaded up on his forehead. When he finished injecting himself, I saw the affects of the heroin grip him immediately, the long "nod." I knew at that precise moment that I had to make some drastic changes in my life or what I just witnessed in front of me may just as well be me in the years to come. I had literally arrived at that fork in the road regarding my life and it was time to choose a path to travel down (the streets and the hustle, or an honest living, no matter how difficult and long the road). With a harsh reality check from Danny, I knew I needed a job; I needed to get off of the block. I knew what side of the fork in the road that I was now going to travel down.

Back at the house that I slept in, no longer with my aunt, a friend from the "New Projects" in Plainfield said, "True I can get you hired at my job if you're serious about working." She was standing right in front of my father's house. I told her to wait there while I ran across the street to get a pen and a piece of paper out of Tonya's mother's house where I kept my things to write down the information. God, again watching over me, when I crossed the street to head towards Tonya's house, the police, the patty wagon, and the narcotics unit were pulling up in front of my father's house; it was a raid! The police and "narc's" (narcotics police) jumped out in force and headed towards the front door with a battering ram. With one swing of the battering ram the front door was busted open.

Like with any raid, the police ravaged the house. I immediately continued to Tonya's house and changed my clothes so that the police would not recognize me from the outfit that I had on leaving the house. I watched while the police took away everyone in the house, and needless to say I never did get the phone number for that job offer (it was the last thing on my mind). Luck on my side, I didn't chalk it up to the game. The odds were astronomical that at that exact moment in time, I would be walking across the street and the narcotics unit and uniformed police were but mere seconds away from raiding the house I lived in.

Night fell and I stayed at Tonya's house; I told her that we had to get out of Plainfield soon, otherwise the streets were eventually going to catch up with me; I had been lucky one too many times. I feel that God removed me from harm's way that day of the raid because I chose in my heart following Danny to change my life around, again beating astronomical odds. My childhood friend Keith Bilal would remind me of the danger that I was putting myself in on the block as he would come around John Street and play the voice of reason, purposely pointing out the wrong that I was doing and that I was "much better than the hustle." He would cut through my harden exterior with words that made a valid point (he would eventually become a career police officer in Atlanta, Georgia).

I did some soul searching and realized that I had a solid option (that right "fork" in the road), one that could benefit Tonya, our daughter, and me; it would allow us to get married, put a roof over our heads, and medical care. Looking back, there was just one time in my life up to that point when people actually viewed me with pride versus disgust or as some type of street thug, and that was when I wore the uniform for Air Force Jr. ROTC in high school. It was at that moment that I decided to go into the United States Air Force. I tried to put the many demons from my past at bay as I took the steps to go forward with joining the Air Force. Life had become so much bigger than me with the birth of my daughter; I knew in my soul that it was time to leave Plainfield, New Jersey and to "grow up." Instead of taking years to get in position to marry Tonya, it would be mere months before I would be ready; however, I had to do one thing, pass the entrance exam for the armed services.

Downtown Plainfield had an armed service recruiting station; Staff Sergeant Lier was the Non-Commissioned Officer for the Air Force. I told him that I wanted to join the Air Force. Oddly, it felt like home when I walked into his office; maybe Lieutenant Colonel Rubel of my high school Jr. ROTC program saw more in me than I knew at the time and that is why he spent so much time on me.

My recruiter asked me when I would like to take the Armed Service Vocational Aptitude Battery (ASVAB) test. I told him that I would like to have a few weeks to study for the test. Upon leaving his office, I went and purchased an ASVAB study guide, the key to passing the test. Filled with excitement, I concentrated on nothing else besides studying for the ASVAB test. Tonya's mother allowed me to stay at her house and sleep in the living room on the couch as I prepared for the exam. She knew I truly wanted to change my current situation and marry her daughter. I could no longer stay in my father's home; it was still busy with unwanted traffic from the hustle, even after the raid. Besides, the lights and water were still not on and I didn't want to study by "candle light."

Not having a backup plan, everything was riding on me passing the ASVAB. I knew that the one thing that I could count on was my book smarts if ever I needed to come through by my own hand, this was it. I had survived abuse, isolation, the streets and psychological pain. I knew one thing, I would not be denied. I focused intently on every aspect of the ASVAB test, understanding the nuances of the exam. When the time came to take the exam, the recruiter took me to Somerville, New Jersey for testing.

When I began the exam, I felt like I had done the studying to pass it. I went through each portion of the exam methodically. When I walked out of the examination room my recruiter asked me how I felt. I told him that I believed that I passed the exam. Oddly I kept asking myself what I would do if I didn't pass. I felt like I was at the end of my rope with one hand holding on to it; so much was riding on me passing the test.

Once we returned back to the recruiting station, my recruiter asked me to have a seat outside of his office. As I sat there, recruiters from the other branches of the service poked their heads out of their office. Each of them were letting me know that if I did not score high enough to get into the Air Force that they would be glad to have me in their branch. Besides the Air Force, I really did not want to go into another branch; I prayed that I had the qualifying score! When the recruiter called me back into his office, he said, "Sean, I have your score back." I sat there with a lump in my throat and said, "Did I pass?" He said, "Congratulations you've made the qualifying score to join the Air Force!" I tried to play it cool, but I was over taken with emotion, understanding the magnitude of the moment.

I knew, pending the qualifying physical, I was going to get a fresh start at life. The next question my recruiter asked me was when did I want to leave for basic training? I said, "tomorrow." He laughed and said that it doesn't happen that fast. I asked him what jobs I qualified for. He said that with my scores and how fast I wanted to leave that "Open General" would be my best bet (which gave me an immediate pool of job choices to select from). I said no problem. I would have dug ditches at that point in my life for the Air Force if that's the job that they would have given me. After qualifying for my medical clearance and completing my entrance paperwork, I was given my ship out date of October 14, 1988.

With my immediate future looking better, Tonya and I set a wedding date. True to their word, both of Tonya's parents agreed to let me marry their daughter (even if it was faster than they anticipated) and we would be leaving for a new life in the Air Force. We immediately went into planning mode for the wedding. September 17th was the date that we set and it was already July. I told my partners from the block (The JSP) that I was leaving; many just didn't believe it, and many said that, "You couldn't pay me to go into the military, screw that!" However, some told me that it was a good move and that if they had graduated from high school or not caught a charge that they would have gone into the service too. Many of my partners from the block were very intelligent young men; chance and circumstance put so many black youth at risk during that time period. I was so thankful that I went back to high school.

To everyone that took part and encouraged me to go back to school, let me say thank you.

With the wedding day finally at hand, it was time for the bachelor party. It was "epic" (a term that is used these days), everyone showed up to the party. I combined my party with an allied block member's birthday party from the "Honcho's from Third," Gary Green. We rented what appeared to be the entire hotel (individual rooms); even people from rival blocks showed up that night. Ironically, there were no fights and everyone got along. My pockets were stuffed with gift money and everyone showed their love in one way or another.

I remember being so drunk that I could barely stand on my feet after a while. The cops eventually showed up because the party was growing out of control, but it was impossible to lock everyone up. The cops wanted to know who the groom was and eventually I found myself being questioned by the police. Luckily my cousin "Beef," who did not drink or do anything "questionable," watched over me for the most part of the night. Even telling the police that I was getting married in the morning and then shipping off to basic training for the Air Force in the weeks to come.

The cops verified that I was the groom and told me that I needed to "sleep it off." I gave my cousin the money that was given to me that night as a gift from everyone, and told him to keep it for me until the next day; he was a groomsman in the wedding. At that point all I could do was fall asleep on the bed but the party continued on; it had become its own entity.

To this day people still talk about that night. There are no words to put to the pages of this book that could remotely describe the events of that evening. I'll simply say that Plainfield, New Jersey showed me a lot of love and I'll never forget it.

The following morning I was out, fast asleep. By chance, P-Love from John Street woke me up and said "True" wake up, today's your wedding day! Hung over badly, I made my way to my feet and woke my cousin Beef up and asked him to take me to get dressed for the wedding. Before leaving the hotel room, I looked back at P-Love and said "you are going to make it to the wedding, right?" he said, "Yes, I wouldn't miss it for the world!" Not only would he miss the wedding, but he would also spend two straight days in the hotel recovering from the party. We laugh about it still today; he always says "man was I hung over bad!" Who paid for the room and the number of days remains a mystery to this day. But, I do know he was not at the wedding or the reception.

Now dressed and at the church, my wedding party consisted of 10 groomsmen: Fats, Divine, Haleem, Jonel, my cousin Beef (as previously mentioned) and Brian to name a few, and ten bridesmaids. My brother Kirk, always by my side, would serve as the best man. It was a packed church. All of Tonya's relatives were in attendance and my relatives from my father's side were there. I had a few of my mother's relatives who attended the wedding, to include my Aunt Cynthia who was there to support me on my big day.

Tonya and I exchanged our wedding vows and we headed to the reception. Her father had made sure that it was a wedding befitting of a king and queen, to include the stretch Mercedes Benz and breathtaking wedding reception. We partied like there was no tomorrow and for the most part, the entire John Street Posse and many of my partners from throughout the city showed up to the reception to congratulate me on getting married. I believe Tonya and I were the first of our age group to tie the knot. It was a memorable day, one I'll never forget.

Tonya and I did not take a honeymoon; instead we went to the Embassy Suites and stayed there for a week. Tonya was so young as a mother, and now a bride, I prayed that her faith in me was well founded. Inside I was still dealing with a lot of emotional issues from my past but I knew that I had to bury it. We had amassed enough money between the bachelor party and the wedding reception to set us up with the essentials for our new life initially, to include a down payment on my first car, a 1988 Ford Tempo that had no air-conditioning, power windows, or rear defogger. But hey, I still loved my first car . . .

With some of the proceeds from the wedding, I paid my traffic tickets off and made a surcharge payment schedule with the state of New Jersey in order to be allowed to drive once again.

Tonya's mother allowed us to stay with her until the time came for me to head off to basic training. I made it a point to stay off of the "block" going into the last few weeks before I headed off to basic training. I did not want to get caught up into anything that could jeopardize me going into the military. I knew it was time to leave the streets alone. I told Tonya that I would not fail in basic training. I knew what was at stake. Heading to basic training, I had only one fear, one that I did not share with the medical staff at the Military Entrance Processing Station—my night terrors! I prayed that I did not wake up in the middle of the night screaming as I relived an episode of my battered youth deeply rooted in my subconscious as I slept.

Chapter 11

Pleased to Meet you, Uncle Sam

A month after my wedding, I was off to San Antonio, Texas for Air Force basic training; Tonya drove me to the recruiting station and we said our goodbyes. My new wife's eyes were filled with tears I recall, as I said goodbye to her shortly after our wedding. On the plane ride down, I kept to myself and did not say much to the other guys that were heading down to basic training with me. I really did not know what to expect when I got there. My only thoughts of basic training were from movies that I had seen. However, good, bad, or indifferent I was on my way to meet Uncle Sam. I thought to myself, *how hard could this be?* I would soon find out what being a basic trainee was all about in the United States Air Force.

Once we landed at the airport, it was like a machine. The Air Force had everything in place for us as we departed our aircraft. Walking off the plane and into the terminal, I thought to myself, *it is now or never!* While they collected all of the trainees for transportation, everything seemed to move at a different speed. We were loaded onto a bus and then we headed to Lackland Air Force Base. San Antonio looked so different to me; it was not like home at all. After we pulled up to the receiving station I knew it was "for real." Everything was "hurry up and wait!" "Pick your bags up, now set them down!" "Get heel to toe" behind one another. It was organized chaos . . .

The moment finally arrived when we were to meet our Military Training Instructor, or MTI, otherwise known as the Drill Sergeant! He was a 6'3" chiseled drill sergeant. When he went to introduce himself, he purposely kept his eyes hidden; they were hidden behind the "Smokey the Bear" style hat. Once his head was totally lifted, he had a "thousand yard stare" about him. I thought, *man, this is going to be bad!* He said "the first thing that I want to hear out of your filthy mouths from now on is, yes sir!" I thought that was easy enough on my part. That night we were given a quick meal as "Rainbow's" (that is, not having been issued our military uniforms) and then we were marched back to the barracks for our bay and bed assignments. That night I met recruits from all over the country. Some were from the west coast, some from the mid-west; really they were from all walks of life.

My bunkmate "Mills" that first night was a wreck, his hands were shaking terribly, and he just could not get it together I recall. I tried to help him out the best I could as the chaos of the day was coming to an end. That night I did not sleep much, if at all. I laid there afraid to go to sleep; I did not want to wake up out of a cold sweat. At 5 a.m. sharp, revile sounded off and the T.I.'s were there to ensure that we had as much enthusiasm as they did. To be honest, that first morning was a blur.

While the day unfolded, we were given tons of shots and we in-processed to the Military Personnel Flight. Once we were done in-processing, it was time to get our uniform and haircuts. I'm thinking *yes, a little off of the sides and tighten my fade haircut up*. However, once I sat in the chair, there were no requests for the type of haircut I wanted; instead it took all of about one minute for them to give me a standard buzz cut. It did not bother me so much as it did the white guys; many of them had long hair. After that we were issued our uniforms and we were no longer "rainbows;" we were Airman Basics and we all looked alike.

When we got back to our flight room as members of the 3711th Training Squadron (The Blue Marines), we were shown how to fold our clothes into painstaking little squares, not easy at all, and place them into our clothing drawers. However, before that, we had to stand up and let the rest of the Flight know what part of the country we came from. Each Airman stood up and gave their information and I became nervous, knowing that I had never spoken in front of a crowd before. When my time came, I stood up and said my name is Sean Hoggs from Plainfield, New Jersey. My T.I. looked at me and said "Jersey huh? I have a plan for you, Airman Basic Hoggs." I thought, *man, I've only been here for a minute and this guy has it out for me already*.

When everyone finished up telling who they were and where they were from, I noticed that he had singled out three other Airmen besides me. When he released us to go back to our respective bay for the night, he called the four of us into his office. He said, "Gentlemen, place these badges over your left pocket, and congratulations on being selected as a Squad Leader!" One was chosen as a Dorm Chief (the unlucky soul that had to run everything). In my mind, I was like, what! It was the Lieutenant Colonel Rubel scenario playing out all over again.

That same night, we had a "shake-down;" that is, where all of your civilian personal items are placed on your bed before they were locked up in the storage closet until graduation. The T.I. would make his way around to each bed with the Team Member (second in command that was his assistant). When the team stopped at my bed, I really did not have anything that I thought was of a concern, but I was wrong. When he dug through my items he picked up a particular picture. It was a picture of me and some of the John Street Posse members, (B-Lord, Fats, Dino, Goot, Romeo Black, Spoony, P-Love and Star to name a few) standing on the corner of 4th and Plainfield Avenue back home in New Jersey. It was their way of showing me some love when I left the block, but more important, we had taken tons of "block pictures" like that before by none other than "Pop," a fixture to Plainfield, New Jersey and a street historian of sorts with his gritty photos of everyday life in the city. To me (at that time) I really didn't think that the picture was that big of a deal. The picture had me kneeling down with a .45 Caliber Pistol between my legs, surrounded by the rest of the John Street Posse. Looking back, I can admit that it was a bad move.

My T.I. looked at me and asked, "Airman Basic Hoggs, are you some type of gang member?" I said no hesitantly, "not really." He said, "Well explain this picture to me," and "who are all of these guys?" I told him that they were my friends from back home, members of the John Street Posse (a gang in my TI's eyes, but not in mine). He then wanted to know whose gun I was holding—mine, or someone else's. I told him that the gun belonged to someone else, which it did. During that time it was very common to take those types of pictures. After all, my gun was a black .25 Caliber Pistol, and now history; I no longer had a need for it, stashed away in a crack house that would later be demolished and removed, the streets were behind me. Looking back, truthfully I should have never had a gun in the first place.

That night I thought I was on my way back home to Plainfield, that fast, as something that I perceived as trivial (a photo) was actually a big deal to those who had never grown up around violence, drugs, gangs or posses (it was everyday for me). Holtz, who was from Los Angeles and in my squad, actually understood what I was saying. Like me, he was no stranger to gang/street violence, drugs, and guns. I told him that I hope that I get to stay and finish basic training. I did not want to return home to a new wife that I had promised that I would see it through. I was worried!

My T.I. said that he would have to look into it all and see if the picture could be a basis to have me discharged and sent home. I thought "Man! I fought this hard to get to this point and a picture, one photo, could do it all in." Needless to say I didn't sleep that night. The next morning came and we ate breakfast, my T.I. said that he would need to see me in his office immediately. I kept thinking to myself, what am I going to do if I have to go back home to the block? After all, this was "all or nothing" for me.

I did my reporting instruction to get into my Team Chief's office (just learned the day before). He said, "Enter!" He cut right to the chase, and said "Airman Basic Hoggs you will be able to remain in basic training; however, your picture is being confiscated and you will not be getting it back." In my mind I thought, man, keep the picture, as long as I did not have to go back to New Jersey as a failure to my wife and child. I did know that I was lucky and I am thankful for the decision makers who let me remain in Air Force basic training.

During the weeks that passed by, I looked forward to receiving letters from my wife, Tonya; she would douse the letters in perfume and it made for an amusing time at mail call by my T.I. The Flight fast became a cohesive unit and the T.I. would put any Airman that needed some "tough love" from the Flight into my squad. I became a focused no-nonsense Airman who just wanted to graduate and get out of basic training.

With the weeks passing along, everything became a routine for the Flight. We were becoming extremely efficient, not only in drill, but in our dorm duties and everyday tasks. At the end of a training day, we were able to take care of our uniforms, take showers, cleanup the sleeping area and have the dorm in inspection order in no time. We were so efficient that when it became time to compete for "Honor Flight," we felt really confident going into the competition. Honor Flight meant that you were the best Flight amongst all the training flights that were assigned to your squadron. As we entered into the competition, we were also finding out what our jobs would be in the military and where our first bases of assignments were going to be.

My assignments technician said that I would be assigned as a Material and Facility Specialist. I said "what is a Material and Facility Specialist?" The technician said "you are going to Base Supply." I thought, *easy enough, no problem; I have a job in the United States Air Force and that is all that really matters*! I was so proud at that moment. I then asked where was my technical training school for my job going to be. The technician said that I did not have a technical school to attend and that I would be going directly to my first duty location. I thought, *great, even better than I hoped for*. It would allow me to return home earlier than I thought to get Tonya and that we could start our new life.

Immediately, I called Tonya on the phone that day when we were permitted to call, and told her that I'm going to be working in base supply. Tonya was just as happy as I was; she was ready to start her new life as my wife. Tonya, excited, asked me where we were getting stationed at, I told her K.I. Sawyer Air Force Base, Michigan. She said "Michigan?" I said yes, we will be close to Detroit and it will be just like home.

Now back with the Flight, we got the results of the Honor Flight competition. The T.I. had us all gather in the day room, he said "I have some news for the Flight regarding the competition." We sat there hanging off of his every word. "Congratulations, you have won the Honor Flight competition!" We erupted into a loud cheer and we stood up and congratulated one another. Winning the competition would allow us to watch television (yes, by that point a television was worth its weight in gold), it also allowed us to stay up a little later, and lastly, it allowed us to have a few extra treats at dinner (it was the small things that mattered most). We had done the impossible and for the first time in my life I was a part of an effort that was greater than me; I will never forget it.

Graduation day was finally at hand. My Aunt Cynthia and Tonya had flown down for the ceremony. My chest was full of pride and I could not wait for Tonya and my Aunt to see me in my uniform. I was still riding a natural high from wining the Honor Flight award, but I was even more proud that I started and finished basic training, without incident (barring the picture ordeal) along with having made some friends along the way. As my Flight did its "Pass-in-Review" as an Honor Flight at graduation during the parade, I thought nothing could stop me now.

Now back in New Jersey briefly, Uncle Sam had given me 15 days of advance leave. When I returned home, Poncho, AKA "P-Love," picked me up from Newark airport (which he would do for years to come). It was good to see a familiar face from the block after basic training. Poncho could not believe that I had gone through with it jokingly (joining the military). We were like a hand in glove before I left for the military, but he supported my decision.

In the days to come, I hung out in the streets, but I was ever so cautious because I knew what was at stake, even getting walked in on by the police at a hotel room party. As the cops asked for identification I handed him my new Air Force ID card. He looked at it and smiled and said that it was best if I left the party and that I did not want to get an Article 15 back at my duty station for the events in New Jersey; not knowing that I hadn't even reported to my first base yet. How would I have explained that one to my new leadership upon arrival? "Hi I'm Airman Basic Hoggs reporting in and I have charges pending in New Jersey that I need to tell you about." Not good!

Luck would have it that the police officer went on to tell me that he was in the Air Force Reserves, so he was giving me a break (thank God!). I told him that I just got back from basic training and that I was just hanging out with some of my old friends in the room. Looking back, me having Airman Basic on my identification card let him know that I just entered the military with less than 6 months of active duty time. I knew he had given me a break so I took his advice and headed out from the party while the police searched and cleared the room out.

Chapter 12

A Winter Wonderland

The time had finally arrived for Tonya and me to leave Plainfield. We jam-packed our car with as much as we could, as we were off to start our new life together. Initially thinking that we would be heading to a place close to Detroit, we felt comfortable knowing that we would be in a place that looked like home. However, mapping out our route to Michigan, we realized that we would be some eight hours away from Detroit, in a place called the "U.P.," or Upper Peninsula of Michigan. Upper What?

Tonya's mother had agreed to care for Tyneshia, our daughter, while we went to our first duty station to set up our home. As we drove towards the U.P., Tonya and I were excited that we were finally getting out on our own, and I was excited to have a new lease on life. We talked about what seemed like everything as we headed towards our new horizon. Once we made it to the Michigan border, we knew we were eight or nine hours away from the Air Force base.

We made our first stop initially to get gas. Me being a Jersey guy, I pulled up to the gas station and I looked for the attendant to come out and pump our gas—standard practice in the state of New Jersey and the Tri-State area. I must have sat there for 30 minutes or more, growing more and more angry as no one showed up to pump my gas. I finally went into the gas station and asked "if anyone felt like pumping my gas today?" The cashier looked at me strangely and asked if I was injured or was there a problem at the pump? I told the attendant, no! The attendant asked what was the pump number and how much gas did I want? Then it dawned on me, I had to pump my own gas; it was the first time I had ever experienced having to pump my own gas in my life.

I told the attendant that I wanted to fill up and then I went back outside to fill my car up with gas. Tonya, being 18 years old and never having pumped her own gas either, and me never having pumped my own gas before, made for quite the adventure as we both looked like we were completely lost as we tried to fill the car up. It made for one of those comical just-between-us moments in a marriage that we will never forget! Looking back I'm sure the gas attendant got a good laugh out of the two fools from New Jersey that never pumped their own gas before, but hey, there's a first time for everything. From that point on, we were good to go regarding pumping our own gas. In fact, Tonya and I got a good laugh out of it in the end as we headed towards the Air Force base.

While traveling north through Michigan, I began to notice that the scenery was starting to change around us. The state went from looking urban as we drove past Detroit and Flint to looking more like a scene out of a wilderness movie. I prayed that my destination, my first duty assignment, did not look like this. The time came when we reached the Mackinac Bridge; it was the bridge that connected the lower part of Michigan to the Upper Peninsula. Back in New Jersey, I must have had crossed the George Washington Bridge hundreds of times in my life going back and forth to New York City, but nothing could have prepared me for this bridge. It literally was the largest bridge that I had ever laid my eyes on! As we began to cross it, Tonya panicked. I tried to keep my composer in front of her but I was literally in a cold sweat myself!

Driving farther and farther onto the bridge, the wind began to blow even harder as we crossed it. It felt like at any second the wind was going to pick up the car and toss us over the edge. Needless to say, but it was a long way down! I told Tonya to close her eyes, and I did the best I could do to cross the bridge without killing us. Once we made it to the other side, I told Tonya to relax, we were safe. It was an eye-opener for us both, and it served as our welcome to the Upper Peninsula of Michigan.

Thinking that we were close to the base, we pulled over at a restaurant to get some food and gas. When we went into the restaurant the cashier welcomed us, but oddly she said, "Oh, you must be going to the base." I said, "Yes we are." With her making that statement without me looking at the map, I thought we were close to the base. I asked her "How far it was to the base?" She said, "About two and a half hours away." I was puzzled. I thought *how would she know that we were going to the base if it was two and a half hours away?* Then it dawned on me when I looked around—we were literally the only black people in the restaurant. We were getting eye balled by everyone. I knew then that there were not a lot of black people in the Upper Peninsula of Michigan. Especially if she was able to surmise that we were going to the military base and it was two and a half hours away! I asked myself, what was I in for?

Heading toward the main highway that crossed the peninsula, US Route 2, we were greeted by a vicious crosswind and snowstorm that was unmerciful. To a guy from New Jersey, having never driven in winter "white out" type conditions like this (unable to see anything because of the heavy snow storm), I was terrified. I could barely see the road or traffic signs, and the white out didn't help at all. I thought to myself, why? Thank God that I filled up by the restaurant with gas; Lord knows, had we run out of gas, we probably would have died in those blizzard conditions if we sat on the side of the road.

Finally nearing the base, the sign read "K.I. Sawyer Air Force Base, 7 miles." We had arrived at our destination and not a moment too soon. The road trip to get to the Air Force base after the bridge was an incredible journey to say the least! When I pulled up to the gate, I was not exactly sure what to do. I gave my military identification card to the gate guard and told him that I was just reporting to the base. It was nighttime and he gave me directions to the military lodging. Once I checked in and got my room, Tonya and I got settled in for the night after eating a quick meal.

The next day, I woke up early thinking that my sponsor (the person who was assigned to me to get me acclimated to the base) would show up at my room to take me to my new job, but no one ever showed up that first day. I thought, maybe they gave me the day off after the long drive to get to the base. Eventually I got out of my uniform and put back on my street clothes, telling Tonya that they must have given me the day off. Being new to the military, I just did not know any better. This would go on for a few days until I finally called my unit and said that I was in lodging. They sent my sponsor to pick me up and bring me to the squadron (my new job). Once there, I met my new boss and my co-workers. When I looked around, I noticed that I worked in a huge warehouse with boxes upon boxes stacked on the shelves. I thought to myself, is this UPS? That would not be the last shock for me that day as I got settled in to my new unit.

Being newly married and with a dependent, naturally Tonya and I looked forward to getting our first home together. After in-processing the squadron, my sponsor took me back to get Tonya so that we could go and look at some homes off base, as we could not move on base right away per the housing office. I thought, no big deal; a home is a home, right . . . Wrong!

Driving up to the place where "most of the young married Airman that were waiting for on-base housing lived at" according to my sponsor, I didn't know what to make of what I was looking at. My sponsor said "here's where you'll find a cozy mobile home for the two of you and your daughter that's affordable on your salary." Being a "City-Slicker" from New Jersey, and having never seen, let alone live in a mobile home, I had no idea what in the world he was talking about. I looked at Tonya and said, "What is that?" Tonya being from down south and very familiar with mobile homes was all too anxious to take a look said, "That's where our new home is" with a big smile. She was just fine with it, but for me, I thought I was in the Twilight Zone or something!

Eventually we would do all of the paperwork and get settled into the place we now called home (the mobile home). We were able to furnish our mobile home on a high-interest credit card by a company that made it all too convenient for military members to get approved (not knowing any better, or really understanding credit having used cash for everything back home). As I started my new job, Tonya turned our mobile home into a "home" with her touch. I just was not used to walking into my living room, dining room, and kitchen all in one step. Not to mention, I could walk back into the bedroom with maybe 10 steps. To say that the mobile home was small would be an injustice! On top of that, I learned about lake effect snow. That's where it would snow and then you would get double the amount of snow by way of the moisture absorbed off of the lake that was next to the mobile home park. In fact, it was so cold that you could literally spit in the air and it would freeze before it hit the ground.

Outside of our mobile home and everyone else's, I noticed a mop handle-like pole by the front door with a stuffed like sock on the end of it. I thought to myself, why's that there? Well I would find out fast, it snowed like crazy in the UP. The pole was used to find your car in the morning because the snowstorms, coupled with the lake effect snow and drifts, completely covered your vehicle from time to time. It made it impossible to find your vehicle unless you had one of those "snow poles." Now, you could have had an idea where your vehicle was, but I assure you finding it was another story without that snow pole. I became a master at finding my vehicle and digging it out. Yes, it snowed that often and that hard, not to mention the bone chilling cold! It was an eye opening experience for a city kid from New Jersey to say the least.

Note: At 32 degrees Fahrenheit, you would actually find yourself sweating and wearing shorts outside because it was warm to you because it normally stayed well below freezing. You would even take your grill out at 32 degrees because you considered it a "heat wave." It was that cold up there.

When I began to work my new job, it was clear that it was a UPS-style job. In the morning, I would come in for a quick daily operations brief, then load my truck up with packages, and make my deliveries throughout the base, and yes it was freezing. It was so cold that you had to wear special cold weather gear to go outside to work. To be honest, it did not take a lot of skill to do the job at all, but it paid the bills. I thought to myself, *I hope that there is more that I can do besides deliver packages all day and sweep the warehouse when I'm done for the day.*

My section was run by a Technical Sergeant (E-6) and Staff Sergeant (E-5). The E-6 was a Vietnam-era throwback that was at the end of his career, and the E-5 was his right-hand man. I'll call the E-5 Blake for the sake of this book. Blake made sure that the shop ran with precision. Truth be told, it was as if he ran the entire show. For the most part, my shop consisted of a bunch of hunters and fishers who loved the outdoors. Then there was me, the guy from New Jersey who had absolutely nothing in common with the outdoorsmen. It fast became the case that I would not be a part of the 'good 'ole boys club' when it came to being "one of the guys."

Growing up in the city never exposed me to hunting, camping, snowshoeing, snowmobiling, or anything like that. I even tried my hand at some of the different activities to fit in, but it just was not my cup of tea. They even got me to try some venison (deer) after tricking me, but after tasting it, it was a onetime experience for me; I knew it was not beef, like they claimed. The guys that were a part of my shop asked to be stationed there because of the outdoor environment. Me, I wanted no part of the Upper Peninsula and I did not ask to be stationed there. I was beginning to think that I had made a big mistake by joining the Air Force.

I was frustrated; I didn't know what else to do to fit in. I showed up to work on time, with a pressed uniform every day, but no matter what I tried, I simply was not accepted. I would find myself sitting out in the break area alone, as I had nothing to offer up in any of the shoptalk. Everything involved some type of outdoor activity that I just was not a part of. To them, I fast became a "troop with an attitude." In actuality I was a "city slicker" to a bunch of outdoorsmen.

Blake would be relentless with his attention to me. I just could not win or catch a break with my section leadership. I was beginning to be written off as a troubled troop with an attitude. Blake would always say, "Airman Hoggs you are on your way back to New Jersey," and he would have the most disgusted look on his face. My initial enlisted performance reports painted me out to be a lazy troop that needed constant direction. However, knowing that I had a wife and child to feed, I was never late to work and I was always the last to leave.

I could not believe what was happening, but then again it was the story of my life, nothing easy and always the Bastard Child. I even raised my concerns up the chain, but who was going to listen to an Airman with relatively no time in the Air Force? I knew the reports were wrong, but in the end even if I continued to fight it, I would lose out.

At night I would come home and tell Tonya that I think I might get kicked out of the military because I was not fitting in (failure to adapt, [to the good 'ole boy clique] truth be told). When I tried to talk to some of the guys in the shop, I would always get looked at like I had three heads or something. It was very apparent that I was not "one of the guys." The other troops that looked like me oddly worked different shifts and were either separating from the Air Force soon or moving on to a new base. Being a young Airman, I was not going to be able to work a swing or a midnight-shift like them because I did not have the proper skill level yet.

After work, I found myself spending a lot of time in the dorms with some of the guys from the other squadrons and flights not from my unit. Although I had left the means streets of New Jersey behind me, I fast discovered that there was a sub culture to the base. There were about five or six cliques or groups that hung out together tight, and between them all there were the Hill and the Hole (where the respective dorms were located). Everyone had their claim to their part of the country. I found myself completely caught up in the madness too, foolishly. Everything that I had fought so hard to get away from in New Jersey, was now right at my door step again in some strange way.

Eventually the foolishness would catch up to me and I found myself on the radar of my leadership, and rightfully so this time. I had my fair share of friends, but I had also made my fair share of enemies on the base because of the silly beefs we all had depending on who you hung out with and what part of the country you were from. Tonya was also getting tired of me hanging out as I was married and running the clubs with the guys from the dorms. The walls were definitely coming in on me. My duty section was getting the documentation they needed to have me discharged if I did not straighten up and fly right. I learned fast that "the pen was mightier than the sword." All that I had fought for, all that I hoped to gain in the Air Force was fast becoming a nightmare. Here I am "public enemy number one" and I had no one to blame outside of the job but me!

In July of 1990, Tonya and I welcomed our second child Seantia Felicia Hoggs into the world. She was named after me, thinking that she was going to be a boy and we had not chosen any other name. During the ultrasounds we would tell the doctor that we didn't want to know what the sex was and we kept our fingers crossed in hopes of a boy, but overall a healthy child. Tonya gave birth to our daughter as I sat there watching the incredible experience. This time I was able to be in the delivery room as a married man while comforting the mother of my children; inside I was a nervous wreck. I didn't know whether to say push, or can I help; I was just happy to be there. When we welcomed our newborn into the world there was no "stem on the apple," nonetheless I was a very proud and happy father. As we scrambled to name our new bundle of joy we took my name and put "tia" on the end of it and we had the name "Seantia" (pronounced, Shon-tee-a). Her middle name, Felicia, was derived from one of my best friends in high school that passed away a few years prior to her birth.

It was right around this time that I found out that my brother Jeff from Florida had died; he was only 26 years old. He died as a result of a gunshot wound that left him paralyzed from the waist down. I was a wreck on the inside as one of the most protective, understanding, and caring figures, (although he was living in Florida at the time), in my life was gone. I was numb when I got the call from his wife, Anita. I flew Tonya and the kids back home to New Jersey as I went to Florida to pay my respect to my brother (spending less than 48 hours there as I had no stomach for Amelia, having remembered what she had done to me years back). My main concern at that time was to make sure that my brother's wife had everything that she needed as she dealt with my brother's death. By this point in my life, sadly, I had been to a lot of funerals of friends that had been killed by street violence. However, going to the morgue and seeing my brother on the table with the V-Stitching down his chest rocked me to the core. I simply could not believe he was gone. It made for a long flight back to Michigan. It messed me up bad inside; it pains me to write about it even today.

Back in Michigan and in my self-induced tailspin, I luckily managed to get all of my skill level upgrades and incremented promotions only by the grace of God. Now in my third year of the Air Force, the Department of Defense began to draw down its forces as a result of the Cold War coming to an end. Supply was not retaining as many Airman as they had in the past, which meant that I was not going to get a Career Job Reservation which would have allowed me to reenlist in a year, which meant that I would have to either separate from the Air Force (which I feared) or re-train into another career field (which was just fine by me).

I began looking into career fields that I could retrain into and I came across the Logistics Planner's career field (645X1 back then, now 2G0X1). I chose to pursue that career field as my job of choice to stay in the Air Force. There was only one problem, so had everyone else that worked in my duty section that had to retrain or separate. Unlike them, my initial Enlisted Performance Reports painted an average picture of me at best. However, the other airmen in my shop all had glowing performance reports in comparison to me; they were a part of the "good 'ole boy club." Knowing that, I just knew I was on my way out of the military and back to New Jersey. The window was too tight for me to find and apply for another Air Force career field in time before I had to separate.

At that time, the Bench Stock Flight had another E-6 that I'll call Dan that always had a kind word for me. He knew what I was dealing with in my shop and he would tell me to just hang in there and it'll get better in time. I remember telling Dan that I was going to have to separate and that I was trying to re-train into another career field before I had to get out. Part of the requirement for the Logistic Plans job required me to come in and interview for the job as well as take a writing and speech test at the time. It was like shooting ducks in a barrel for me, because I felt comfortable doing both. That said, the rest of the troops in my shop (in hopes of retraining) took the same test and were interviewed by the same people that I was. I knew at that point upon review of everyone's records in comparison to mine, that I was on my way out the door regarding the United States Air Force.

When the packages and recommendations were sent up for review and approval, the weeks crept by slowly. I told Tonya that more than likely we were going to have to go back to New Jersey and start anew there, which we both knew would have spelled disaster, if not the end for us.

Eventually, we were all notified of the results of the test, interview, and hiring. Thinking that it was a wash for me, I dreaded the moment. I made my way over to the Consolidated Base Personnel Office to hear the bad news first-hand. When the technician handed me my folder, I paused and then opened up the letter inside slowly. It said, "Congratulations on being selected to the Logistics Plans Career Field!" I all but fainted; I actually thought that I had the wrong folder. Ironically, no one else from my duty section (or the Good 'ole boy club) was selected and they were all targeted for separation, I just could not believe it!

In the weeks to come, before I started my new job, I found out that Dan had put a favorable call in for me to let them know that my initial Enlisted Performance Reports were not reflective of who I was as an Airman. Because of that call and my test scores, I made the cut. When I told Tonya that I had been approved for re-training, she was relieved. We both prayed that we didn't have to return to New Jersey to start our life over again. I happily said goodbye to Base Supply forever. Dan S., Thank you again for believing in me, when it was evident that others did not.

Now working in the 410th LGLX office with the other Logistic Planners, it felt real. They welcomed me in and got me settled into my new digs. The first thing that they gave me was my own desk! I remember asking if I had to share my desk with anyone, something we had to do in base supply (a metal one at that). I was told that it was my desk and that I did not have to share it with anyone. Not to harp on the desk, but it was beautiful!

Unlike base supply, this job had an office appeal to it; it had carpet, computers, and a coffee machine to name a few amenities. There were no trucks with boxes to deliver around the base and no warehouse to sweep out daily. No, in this job, it would not be about how well I could deliver packages, wash trucks, or sweep floors, but how well I could handle the day-to-day responsibilities of a "Log Planner" that required my brain power; I welcomed the change.

Once I was done in-processing the squadron and getting settled into my new office, I was assigned to work the Contingency Operations Mobility Planning and Execution System, or COMPES system as it was referred to. It was the computer system that the Air Force used to store logistical data (personnel and cargo) to meet operational plans for the nation regarding K.I. Sawyer Air Force Base and its role (Strategic Air Command base that housed nuclear missiles). Yes, it was an intimidating computer system and I had to learn it; it was a far cry from supply.

At home, Tonya was getting adjusted to my night terrors after three years. At first, she would sleep on the couch at times as I would literally fight my way out of the covers or completely have the bed soaking wet from being in a cold sweat. My subconscious could not escape the many years of abuse from my youth. I eventually had to sit Tonya down and tell her that from time-to-time, it will happen, and I apologized for her having to live with my painful past. Eventually Tonya made her way back to our bed, but I was embarrassed as a husband and even more so a father, as Tyneshia was now living with us.

It was now time for me to attend my first level of enlisted Professional Military Education in the Air Force, Airman Leadership School. Although I had been in the service for a few years up to that point, I still did not clearly understand the "big picture." Even though I was working in a new job, it was just that, a job!

Sitting in Airman Leadership School, I took note of the instructors and their professionalism. Each instructor had a Community College of the Air Force degree and they were the cream of the crop amongst the non-commissioned officer corps—sharp! As the days and weeks passed by, I began to truly understand my piece of the Air Force puzzle. The lessons that were taught about leadership, the Air Force, the mission and my part began to really sink in. I realized that no matter how small a part I played in the Air Force that my contribution in the Air Force contributed to the overall security and defense of the nation.

Like with the Scared Straight Program of Rahway, it was another point of consciousness for me, but this time in my military life. Airman Leadership School would forever change how I viewed and approached my duties in the Air Force. It was no longer "just a job to me;" it was a profession that I would now dedicate my life to. I knew that I would make a career out of the United States Air Force from that point forward.

I no longer concerned myself with the different cliques on base; I concentrated on becoming the best Airman that I could. I became a student of the COMPES computer system that I was charged with operating. My trainer, Staff Sergeant Nate Middleton, would prove to be an expert of the COMPES system and he taught me the tricks of the trade regarding the computer program over the next few years; I fast became an efficient Airman of the COMPES system and a dedicated Airman to the defense of the United States of America. Life became about the Air Force mission.

Chapter 13

Rome is Burning

It was finally time for me to depart K.I. Sawyer Air Force base. The base had been selected for closure by the government. When I received my Permanent Change of Station (PCS) orders, they were to Pope Air Force Base in Fayetteville, North Carolina. My wife was also now pregnant with our third child. To ensure the wellbeing of my wife and my unborn child (per the doctor's orders), I sent Tonya, Tyneshia, and Seantia back to New Jersey while I prepared for the PCS move.

The base doctor recommended that I send Tonya home to come to full term with her pregnancy. The base hospital was being closed because of the base closing, thereby allowing for medical care to be established at home in Plainfield.

In October of 1994, we welcomed our third child, Tizana Sheree Hoggs. She was named after my wife's two best friends while stationed at K.I. Sawyer Air Force Base. When she gave birth to Tizana, I again was a proud father, and I would nickname her "Lady," because the first picture that I got to see of her, she looked like a little woman all wrapped up in her hospital blanket. I felt a sense of comfort knowing that Tonya was back home with her mother and that she did not have to be alone in the delivery room. I would be returning to Plainfield within the next two months to visit Tonya and the children before I headed south for North Carolina; we would also celebrate Christmas together.

Looking at the big picture, I knew that I would have a long journey ahead of me and that I would need some help driving back to New Jersey from Michigan. To help me drive back home in the following months, my old friend Al Pierre had flown into Marquette, Michigan to help me clean the house (now living on base in military housing for some years) and drive back. Like me upon first arriving to the Upper Peninsula in Michigan, he was shocked to see so much snow. I jokingly told him this was not Plainfield, and to expect snow every day here. However, I believe more people were shocked to see him in the Upper Peninsula as he was literally 7'1."

Al Pierre fast became somewhat of a rock star amongst the base personnel. It was good to have him around for those last few months in Michigan before leaving K.I. Sawyer Air Force Base. After passing my final housing inspection and signing out of my unit, Al Pierre and I loaded up my 1992 Honda Accord and we headed to New Jersey. We drove straight through from Michigan to New Jersey, stopping for gas and food only.

Finally back in Plainfield, it was great to see my family, but more important my newborn daughter, "Lady." Because I had some leave saved up (military vacation days), I was able to spend some time at home. Now understanding the Air Force's bigger picture, I revisited my old stomping ground, but I was very cautious when I approached an old familiar fair-weather friend called the streets. John Street was still in full operation; her lure was tempting, very tempting! It would have been all too easy to "flip" (double and even triple) my honest and hard-earned money from the Air Force. But I knew what was at stake if I had done that. A few fast dollars could have easily turned into a lifetime of regret, but the hustle was again calling for my soul, however brief.

Having seen a different way of life in Michigan, and now understanding the bigger picture that I was a part of in the Air Force, and knowing that I was a father of three now, it was easy for me to walk away from the temptress that was again asking me to hold her hand and dance with her (the streets). Many of the hustlers, 5NOI members, and John Street Posse members still showed me a lot of love, but I knew it was time for me to leave.

Dino, a fellow JSP member and cousin to Tonya, offered to help me drive down to North Carolina to my new base. I told Tonya that with my remaining days of leave and house hunting days that I would go to North Carolina first and find our new house then return to New Jersey to pick her and the children up.

Once I found my new home in North Carolina and signed into my new unit, I returned to Plainfield along with Dino to pick up my family. North Carolina was eight hours or so from Plainfield, New Jersey so it was a long day's ride. Unlike Michigan, I enjoyed the entire trip; there were no surprises on the way there or back.

Dino, who I had survived many neighborhood wars with, was a very close friend and a brother-like figure in my life. He drove down with me to North Carolina for a few reasons, one, he said he needed a break from the "block." The other reason, Dino wanted to help me out; he was proud of me making the changes in my life and wanted to help me along in my new journey, to which I am very grateful to this day. We talked about life as we drove to North Carolina, and my

Rottweiler Zeus made himself all too friendly with Dino, licking his ear every time he fell asleep in the car on the way down; it was actually hilarious and Dino and I would crack up every time he did it. Dino and I remain close to this day as I look back on the kind gesture on his behalf.

Once I returned to North Carolina with Tonya and the children, I got them settled in to our new home on Moss-Wood Lane; it was a beautiful Townhouse in a quiet residential neighborhood. It was a far cry from the trailer that we had to live in initially in "K.I. Siberia." I was a Senior Airman at this point, E-4, and my paycheck went a little further in the south. In our new home, Tyneshia and Seantia shared a bunk bed, and Lady our newborn slept in our bedroom in a crib. The weather was beautiful and there were no "snow poles" to be had in the south. As a nuclear unit, we were settled in as a family.

I was excited to start my new job as I had learned so much about the logistics business at K.I. Sawyer Air Force base. Nate Middleton had taught me well regarding the COMPES system and I had fast become somewhat of an expert with it. To note, in each logistics flight in the Air Force, it was safe to say that one or maybe two individuals would be skilled in the complicated and delicate use of the COMPES system.

Stepping into my new flight, I became the COMPES expert for Pope Air Force Base. It was my sole responsibility to handle the logistical aspects associated with the various A-10 and 141 aircraft, units, their manpower and equipment (a daunting task). Unlike Michigan, there was no Staff Sergeant Middleton to bail me out if I made a mistake. This was swim or sink time for me as my leadership placed the deployment machine in the form of the COMPES system squarely on my back. If I failed, the deployment machine failed.

My timing could not have been any better; the base was due for an Inspector General (IG) Headquarters Air Mobility Command Inspection within the next 18 months upon my arrival to the base. My officer-in-charge was Lieutenant Chris De Los Santos. He was a Merchant Marine Academy graduate and had energy to burn. Together, we would prepare for the inspection together. As complicated as the COMPES system was, he was the "brass" for me when units were being difficult with their deliverables as I used him for leverage. Passing the inspection was a must, and there was no margin for error. For a unit to fail an IG inspection spelled certain doom for commanders, as their jobs, to include Wing commanders, could literally be on the line. I felt the pressure as the lieutenant tried to provide me some type of top cover as I prepared the base for the deployment piece of the inspection, their logistical detail data to be precise in COMPES. It would take me literally a year to get everything in order to put the base in a position to pass the inspection regarding their deployment equipment and personnel in the computer system.

Inspection time came and the IG Team rolled in with their team of experts. Each IG member was an expert at his or her discipline handpicked by Headquarters Air Mobility Command. My inspector would be none other than Senior Master Sergeant Ron Turk, who was well known in the logistics career field throughout the Air Force, and he knew how to make the COMPES system "sing." As Lieutenant De Los Santos and I had spent the past year or so getting ready for this moment, we both prayed that our efforts did not go in vain. If we failed the deployment piece of the inspection, the burden would rest squarely on our shoulders regarding the COMPES piece.

When I sat down with the inspector, he meticulously went through all of my paperwork. There was nothing that got past his eye. I could tell that his reputation was well warranted, as he was a throwback senior non-commissioned officer that was strictly about the business of the Air Force and the inspection. He literally never cracked a smile while he was conducting business, keeping a stern poker face that kept me on the edge of my seat the entire time as I looked for any indication on how things were going with the IG inspection. He wanted to see all of the correspondence that I had regarding pilot unit and non-pilot unit coordination, (that is, other bases that used the same equipment and personnel that we did regarding logistical support). I would not know the outcome of the inspection until the report was written. It was the first time that I felt pressure as a logistician, with the responsibility of it all resting on my shoulders. I did not want to let my leadership down, but more importantly, I wanted to show my immediate leadership that their trust in me was well founded, up to this point I had not been a focal point in my career for such a heavy responsibility.

At the Inspector General out-brief, the entire base was there. This is where the inspection results would be given out in front of the entire

Air Base Wing. Not knowing the results of my portion, I sat in the hangar quiet as my inspector gave no indication. As each squadron and their results were named I kept saying to myself, "God, please have let me at least pass this thing." As I had worked tirelessly on the project with Lieutenant De Los Santos, (13- and 14-hour shifts for weeks/months on end at times), for the first time I was at the helm, and my leadership trusted in me to get the job done, I did not want to let them down.

When my unit was displayed on the video screen, each section or Flight received their respective inspection grade. I could barely bring myself to look up at the screen. In my mind, I kept flashing back to base supply at K.I. Sawyer Air Force base and how I was treated there, knowing that I truly had given my all in the shop, yet my performance report said much different; I didn't want history to repeat itself.

Finally the moment of truth was upon me; it was time for my direct function to have its grade displayed; my heart was literally beating out of my chest. When the slide popped up, I slowly glanced at it. I had received an "outstanding" for my overall rating, the highest you could achieve. Lt. De Los Santos and our squadron commander came over and congratulated me on the rating as it was extremely hard to achieve an "outstanding!" It was the first time in my Air Force career, if not my life, that I felt like I accomplished something that entailed a great level of responsibility. My leadership believed in me (especially Lt. De Los Santos, who "went to bat" for me) and I did not let them or me down.

It was now time for the Inspector General Team to name the "Top Performers" of the inspection. These were the troops that were recognized by the inspection team as those individuals who had gone above and beyond in preparation for the inspection. In my opinion, I knew I had worked hard at passing the inspection, but it was an honest day's work no matter how meticulously I approached it. I simply did not feel that I had warranted such an honor, as through my life, my best was just never good enough. In fact, once I knew we had passed the inspection I recall wanting to leave. No one in attendance knew who the recipients of the awards were so we were told to "stand fast" until the Inspector General Results and announcements were complete.

As each name was called off, I was sincerely happy for each individual and team. I knew that they had poured their soul into passing the inspection; we all did. However, there would be but a few who would be recognized, but all deserved to be lauded. Then the impossible flashed up on the screen, it read from "the 23rd Logistics Support Squadron, Senior Airman Sean P. Hoggs has been selected as an Air Mobility Command, Inspector General Outstanding Performer." I just could not believe what I was looking at! It was my first Air Force "pat on the back" as I was both stunned and elated! It still remains one of my fondest memories while serving in the Air Force.

The months passed by after the inspection and I continued to work the COMPES piece of the mobility element. During that time, a new Senior Master Sergeant (SMSgt) was assigned to my overall flight; for the purpose of the book I'll call him "SMSgt D." The moment he entered the shop, the atmosphere changed immediately. He was rough around the edges and he was quick to remind you that he was a "Senior Master Sergeant in the United States Air Force" and that nothing was given to him to make it to this point in his career. Unlike base supply when I was stuck behind the "8-Ball," and after Airman Leadership School, I had dedicated myself to literally becoming the best airman I could be in the United States Air Force. However, SMSgt D. saw things a lot different. No matter how hard I worked and no matter what I did, it just wasn't good enough for him. He would always remind me that we had to be "that much better" (referring to us both being African American in the Air Force) and that I needed to raise the level of my production. By that time, I knew it was about getting the job done and not just about being African American as he put it. I saw one color, Air Force blue, and that was the team I was playing on.

I believe he resented me being from New Jersey, because he would always make references about the "hoods and street thugs" that came from the New York and New Jersey area and that most of the airmen from those areas were nothing but trouble in the Air Force. I couldn't believe what I was hearing but he was a Senior Master Sergeant and I was a Senior Airman, so what could I really do in this instance. I had fought hard to become the respectable airman that I now was and he saw nothing more than a "street hood" in uniform.

While the time passed by serving with SMSgt D., he began to pressure other Airmen in my flight, even inadvertently forcing one Airman to separate who had planned on making the Air Force a career. She just could not take it anymore from SMSgt D. "Ann J." I'll call her, was a phenomenal troop that delivered the mail on every account, yet, she chose to separate because of him. Knowing what I know now, she was a gem that would have done wonders for the Air Force in her career had she stayed in (we remain friends to this day).

No one wanted to be around SMSgt D. Although I had been named Airman of the quarter for the squadron, and was selected as an IG Outstanding Performer, in his eyes it meant nothing. He would be tenacious in his criticism of everything I did; I could not understand what the problem was. I spoke with my immediate supervisor because I feared that, despite all of my best efforts at Pope Air Force base, he was going to try to ruin my career. Up to that point, as an Airman, I literally was performing at an extremely high level according to my superiors. My supervisor assured me that I would be taken care of on my Enlisted Performance Report and not to worry about SMSgt D. Even Lieutenant De Los Santos went to bat for me. I thought to myself; will I ever get a break in life?

When my Enlisted Performance Report came up due, true to his nature, SMSgt D. fought hard to give me an overall "4" Rating on my enlisted report; saying that I was a lazy Airman, and that I didn't deserve anything higher than a "4," [despite my many accomplishments at Pope Air Force base]. An overall 4 rating would have a negative effect on my potential promotion selection and it would paint a horrible picture of me that simply was not true. I felt like the Bastard Child once again; here it was that I gave my heart and soul to the Air Force mission and this was the reward I was going to get from him.

True to their word, my inner office leadership "circled the wagons" around me and made sure that my report reflected the highest rating of a 5, and even the Group Commander (a "Full Bird" 0-6 Colonel) added in his comments, supporting my efforts at Pope Air Force Base. Simply put, the "brass" along with my immediate supervisor made sure that the right thing was done on my behalf.

A byproduct of hard work and studying, I was selected for promotion as a Non-Commissioned Officer at the rank of Staff

Sergeant; it further validated my belief in the Air Force and its vast opportunities. Despite SMSgt D.'s best efforts to derail my Air Force career, the Air Force saw fit to promote me (and yes it was bitter sweet!). I was also named Air Combat Command's (ACC) Logistics Plans and Programs Specialist of the year; a huge honor that I was extremely proud of, as this award placed me as the best Airman amongst my peers across the various units in the country that supported (ACC).

After being selected for promotion and receiving my award, I knew that I would most likely be getting an assignment, but to where I did not know. It was also during this time that I was growing extremely close to my grandmother on my father's side. We would talk for hours at a time on the phone and when I would come home on leave she would pass me family heirlooms to be the custodian of.

In fact, the first U.S. Air Force Commendation Medal that I was awarded I gave it to her because it meant the world to me, just as she did. She shared how proud she was of me being in the Air Force and that meant everything to me. My grandmother (Nana) was a very prominent and influential woman in Plainfield, and her words spoke volumes. I knew upon her approval that I was on the right track (or fork in the road) regarding life.

In time, my orders finally flowed down; I was going to be stationed at Osan Air Base, Republic of Korea. This assignment was considered a "remote" assignment, which meant that I could not take my family along with me. I would have to find a way to break the news to my spouse, which was no easy task. In a 20-year military career it is understood that at some point within in those 20 years that you do a remote assignment. I did not expect my remote tour so soon in my career. However, it was what I signed up for and I made no bones about it. I finally told Tonya of the impending assignment and we prepared our family for the year-long separation.

Before leaving for Korea, three significant things happened; the first absolutely stunned me. As I sat home after work this particular day I got a phone call from Lieutenant De Los Santos; he said that Colonel Pesola wanted to "speak to me directly," I said "what for, Sir?" Foolishly, I actually thought that I was going to be separated from the military at that point for some reason unbeknownst to me. I thought SMSgt D. had finally found a way to send me packing to New Jersey.

The LT said, "You will have to speak with the Colonel directly;" I cautiously waited to hear the Colonel's voice on the other end of the phone.

When the Colonel finally said hello he asked me, "Is this Senior Airman Sean Hoggs, the Department of the United States Air Force Logistics Plans and Programs Specialist of the Year?" I said "no way, who is this, Mickey Mouse?" and the Colonel said, "Sean, this is really me, not Mickey Mouse, and that this is not a joke. You are the United States Department of the Air Force Logistics Specialist of the Year and I'm personally calling to congratulate you." Needless to say, I just could not believe it! I apologized for my insubordination over the phone but the Colonel chuckled and said he understood. It was not every day that a Colonel would call you directly as an airman.

I was the top Airman in the world (the equivalent of being an undisputed world champion for my weight class in boxing, Airman Category); it was inconceivable to me, the Bastard Child! I had poured everything into Pope Air Force base and the deployment element, and I was extremely thankful that my leadership believed in me enough to submit me for the award. It also put SMSgt D. at bay; he must have figured that if The Department of the United States Air Force selected me as the best in the world at what I did, who was he to argue with that (I say he never looked past his bias of troops from urban areas, the inner cities to be exact). He never did congratulate me on the honor, but he was no longer a threat to my career!

I offer this observation: If SMSgt D. would have been a mentoring figure to me, I would have appreciated his attention, but it was the exact opposite. He was arrogant and lacked humility at his senior position in comparison to the remarkable Sr. NCOs that I would come to know in my 24-year military career!

Following the announcement, the base newspaper did an article on me and I framed it; it hangs in my house to this day. My picture was also placed in the Pentagon that year on its Wall of Honor as the top Logistician for the United States Air Force (Airmen Category). Humbly, it remains one of the most proud moments of my life!

In the military it was a rule that I would come to live by—to never ask to be submitted for any award, medal, or recognition. It should be earned and recommended by your superiors, transparent to you.

The second thing to happen in North Carolina was that my wife was now pregnant once again. I recall her sitting in the bathroom and calling my name. Thinking that she needed some toilet paper, I grabbed some before I went into the bathroom. Sitting there she had tears streaming down her face; I knew that she didn't need any tissue at that point. I asked her "Tonya, what's wrong?" She said, "Sean, I'm pregnant!" I asked her why was she crying and she said that I was not going to be there for the birth of our child.

I told her that we would get through this just like we had gotten through everything else so far in life. I carefully explained to her that she was a military wife and that there were a ton of support agencies in place to help us out during my remote assignment to South Korea. Inside I was very happy that I was going to be a father again. I believe that this is where Tonya really began to understand the hardships of being a military spouse, but she would "circle the wagons" and galvanize the family.

I always wanted a big family, so inside I was elated. I told her to wipe her face off and to stop crying, jokingly calling her a big baby as she smiled slightly. Eventually we put a plan in place that would put her and the children back in New Jersey with her mom so that she did not have to go through the pregnancy alone. It also put her within the proximity of McGuire Air Force Base where she could receive the proper pre-natal care while I was stationed overseas.

With life "a little rain must fall" for everyone, but I had buckets of monsoon rain coming down on me since I was a little child. Before going to Korea, Tonya and I decided to take some leave as a family in New Jersey. It would be the third thing of significance in North Carolina, and one that pains me to write.

Now in Plainfield, New Jersey on military leave before departing for Korea, I found myself enjoying my time at home (around Christmas time). I would be returning to New Jersey in the summer to get Tonya and the children situated before departing for The Republic of Korea. As in the past when I would come home on leave, I would hang out in some of the old spots, but remain cautious as the streets remained a tempting yet dangerous place.

This particular night I was at Tonya's mother's home lying down when we heard a knock on the door. No big deal, so my mother-in-law went to answer it like she had done a thousand times before. When she opened the door it was the police. The officer asked if "Sean Hoggs" was located at this address. She said "yes" and called for me at the door. Immediately I thought the worse, I thought that someone had been killed, shot or locked up. I even foolishly thought that someone might have sold me out from an old bench warrant that I may not have been unaware of. It had been the case in the past when others had used my name during a traffic stop or arrest knowing that I had a clear record. However, I would always have to clear my name one-way or another through military channels; smart on their part! Yes, any time that a police officer knocked on your door in my old neighborhood, it usually meant the worst!

Coming down the steps, I could see the police officer standing there. In the back of my mind, I kept saying to myself, "God I hope this is not bad!" As I addressed the officer, he asked me if I was Sean Hoggs and did I have any identification on me? I said, yes, and I went back up stairs to get my military identification card. When I returned, he verified my information and told me that my military unit needed to speak with me immediately.

My unit had located me off of my leave address on my paper work. It was the first time in my military career that I experienced my unit contacting me while I was on leave; at that point I knew it was military related and that no one had been shot or killed in my family, thank God. I thanked the officer and prepared myself for the call back to Pope Air Force Base. Not sure of the nature of the notification, as the police officer did not know as well, I was still very much on edge. All the police officer was able to tell me was that "I needed to contact my unit."

As directed, I called back to my immediate supervisor at that time, Master Sergeant James Brown. MSgt Brown told me that I needed to return to the base as soon as possible and it would be best if I left my family in New Jersey. Immediately I began to panic, why would they need me to return to the base right way? What had I done to warrant me returning so abruptly? MSgt Brown said he would explain everything once I returned to North Carolina. My mind immediately went into a tailspin as I began to think the worst about something that was still a mystery to me. I explained to Tonya the best I could what was going on, as she was equally concerned, but I told her I would find out the exact nature of everything once I got to the base and let her know. I booked a flight for the next day, with the help of my mother-in-law, and I packed for the trip back home.

The flight was short, but it seemed like it took forever to get to Fayetteville, North Carolina; I did not sleep on the flight at all as my mind raced with so much, I thought the worst; why not? It was the story of my life! MSgt brown was at the airport to meet me, along with Lt. De Los Santos. I knew it was bad at that point. I thought my rights were going to be read to me for something I was still unaware of and that I was headed to military prison.

On the way to the base, Lt. De Los Santos finally told me what I had been brought back off of leave early for. He said, "Sean, there's been a fire." I said "a fire?" He said, "Yes there's been a fire at your town house and it's pretty bad."

Heading towards my home, I kept thinking about all of the family heirlooms that my Nana Lilly had just passed on to me right before she passed away (March 23 of that same year). I thought about the many memories and other mementos that were now destroyed by the fire. For every step I took forward, it just seemed like life was destined to push me back three steps.

When we finally pulled up to my home, the structure was still intact. I thought it couldn't be too bad if the structure is still in place; I would turn out to be sadly mistaken! When I opened the door to walk into the townhouse, the damage was indescribable. Although the structure seemed sound from the outside, the inside was charred; it was as if the townhouse was gutted completely by the fire; I could not believe what I was looking at. Everything was gone, and I mean everything, as if someone tossed a hundred grenades in my home! I was speechless as I viewed the destruction that the fire had caused.

Going through the townhouse room-by-room with the Fire Marshall by my side (now at the home), I could see the devastation in its complete context. Our Rome "wasn't built in a day" as a young married couple, in fact, it had taken years to build our lives piece by piece, item by item, on a limited military salary and in an instant, it was no more. Mere ashes remained; everything was lost. However, I remember the Fire Marshall said something to me that put the fire into perspective. He said, had we been home asleep and not on vacation when the fire started, no one in the house would have survived the fire. At that very moment, I was thankful that my entire family was in

New Jersey; had we been there when the fire started, we wouldn't be here today.

So how did the fire start was the burning question racing through my mind. In the military, it was custom to have your neighbor check your mailbox for you and to place the mail on the kitchen counter or dining room table if you had a trusting and established friendship. That was the case with my neighbors and we trusted them to check on the house and to simply place the mail on the kitchen counter. However, (which would be uncovered by the fire investigation) my neighbors were not only checking the mail, but they decided to wash and dry their clothes for their entire family at the house while we were away on leave/vacation.

The Fire Marshal said that the fire unfortunately started in the dryer (from continuous nonstop use of it) and worked its way throughout the house, a direct result of my neighbors not cleaning out the dryer vent while they dried their clothes. However, I was confused because I had not given my neighbors permission to wash or dry their clothes at my house while I was on leave. They took it upon themselves to use my washer and dryer without asking, and as a result of their poor decision, everything that I possessed was now gone, destroyed by the fire. I had worked so hard up to that point in my life for our little piece of the world, just to have everything go up in flames within minutes. Once again, misfortune had made its presence felt for the Bastard Child; but, I was grateful for one thing, we were all alive! Sometimes you just have to count your blessings.

The next obvious steps were to figure out how we were going to put our life back in order; we literally had nothing but the clothes on our backs. The Red Cross provided some support for us, but it was limited in its resources regarding fire victims. Tonya and the kids were now back in North Carolina, and we lived in military lodging following the fire. Tonya was just as shocked as I was at our neighbors, but even more upset at losing everything we worked so hard for together; she took the fire very hard. We never did show the children the house, and told them that we would be starting over anew, and that all of their toys and belongings were unfortunately lost in the fire.

It was a very hard pill for my young family to swallow. Being a Senior Airman, an E-4, and not making a lot of money in the military (roughly $632.00 bi-monthly before taxes), I couldn't afford renter's insurance. Literally every dime was accounted for regarding our family of five, one way or another. That meant that we would have to rebuild our lives from scratch again, minute-by-minute, day-by-day, week-by-week and month-by-month until it was time for me to leave for Korea.

Just when I thought we were facing an impossible uphill battle as a family, the Air Force family (civilian and military) came to put the pieces back together for us. Unbeknownst to my family and me, the various squadron First Sergeants were taking up a collection on base for my family. They had raised enough money for us to replace literally everything that we had lost in the fire. And with an attorney (that my mother-in-law would pay for), I was able to get the remaining large items (bedroom sets and dining room set) replaced by the neighbors who had caused this all to happen in the first place, (they elected to settle out of court as I pursued suing them).

I was so humbled by the outpouring of generosity by the base that I felt compelled to go to every squadron on base and personally thank them during their "Commander's Call" (where unit personnel met in mass). I shared my story with each unit, and stressed the importance of renter's insurance, but more importantly, I wanted each squadron to know just how filled with gratitude I and my family were, even coming to tears at times; it was a very humbling experience. The Air Force was indeed one big family. The base newspaper (The Tiger Times) shared my story; I wanted to make sure that everyone on Pope Air Force base understood just how thankful we were as a family to the Air Force community.

Resiliency would now have to touch my nuclear family. Yes, I had to experience a lot of trials and tribulation in my life, but it was limited to my personal experience. However, this time life and its trials would place its burdens on everything that my wife and I had worked so hard for. Losing everything taught my family how to embrace resiliency. It was clear that in life, in a moment's notice, everything could be taken away. It taught us to never get comfortable in our station. But more importantly, it brought us together even closer as a family, and it taught my family something more important . . . how to get up again after being knocked down and start over again if life called for it.

A point of emphasis: Life will be filled with challenges; it is what you do at those critical moments that will determine if you will move forward or simply give up. I say, get up and continue to move forward in life. It would have been all too easy to give up after the fire, given my life experiences, but I chose to fight, to be resilient in the face of adversity, even if it meant starting over from scratch as a family, which we did. Don't ever give up.

In the months to follow, I would take Tonya and the children back to New Jersey to get settled at her mother's because I was soon to depart for the Republic of South Korea, that August. Tonya, now pregnant with our fourth child, was in good hands with her mother. On the day I was departing for South Korea, Tonya would drive me to the airport; it would be our first time apart at length since she came to live with her mother in 1986 and the birth of our first daughter. I told her that we would talk to one another and write each other as much as humanly possible. She cried as we said our goodbyes and I wiped her face off and told her that a year would go by in no time; and that before she knew it, I would be back from overseas.

Chapter 14

A World Apart

On the flight over to South Korea, I really didn't know what to expect on the other side of the "pond" (meaning ocean, as we say in the military). I had never been out of the states before and the only references I had to South Korea were the different stories that some of the other GI's had shared. I did as much homework as possible on South Korea before departing New Jersey, but it was truly the case where a "picture would have been worth a thousand words."

Once I arrived on the South Korean Peninsula, after the longest flight that I had ever taken in my entire life, my sponsor greeted me. Getting my room assignment and getting settled in at the squadron was pretty easy. I knew it was a year-long tour and I stayed extremely busy while I was stationed there. In fact, I arrived in South Korea in August of 1997 and I didn't get a day off of work until Thanksgiving weekend.

South Korea was a beautiful country. I was immediately drawn to the sights and sounds that greeted me right outside the main gate. In a strange way, it gave me a sense of home; it reminded me of 42nd Street in New York City with all of the lights, traffic, and excitement. However, South Korea was a far cry from New York and New Jersey, but it made for some great times and great shopping. Korea laid claim to many of the factories that shipped directly to America. The cost of a custom tailored suit was simply unbelievable, "dirt-cheap" in comparison to a handmade suit in the United States. With my family back in the states, I limited my spending and I made sure that Tonya was situated and comfortable back at home with her mother.

In South Korea, there was always an uneasy edge in the air; North Korea was always a real and credible threat and that threat still exists there today. This was made very clear to me when I was getting acclimated to the base and I got to witness the Patriot Batteries that were aligned around the golf course on the north side. Naïvely, I asked my sponsor "What are all of those trucks about?" He told me that they were Patriot Batteries (Anti-Missile Defenses) deployed and manned by the Army, 24 hours a day 7 days a week for the defense of South Korea. I thought "wow, okay, this is for real!" The reality of the threat was also made evident by the war games played by the military installation, as they took a no-nonsense approach to protecting the base, its personnel, and its resources; I quickly understood the gravity of where I was stationed.

Socially, I sought out the local Masonic Prince Hall lodge, having become a Prince Hall Freemason in Eureka Lodge #3, the second oldest lodge in North Carolina. Otis Hopkins Military Lodge #10 would become my home away from home and I would serve as its Master after demitting into the Oklahoma Masonic Jurisdiction while stationed in South Korea. Past Master Herb Hart would be my mentor during my tenure as "Master of the Lodge" and would become one of my best friends in life.

Darrick, George, Jimmy, Moe, James, Tigo, Eric, and Leroy (all Prince Hall Masons) were simply the best friends and fraternity brothers that a man could have on a military installation, as I sat a half a world away from my loved ones. To note, I also had a spiritual awakening; I was baptized as a Christian. I no longer considered myself a Five Percenter (5NOI); I had accepted Jesus Christ as my Lord and Savior.

Every Sunday without exception, we would make dinner for one another and we were extremely close, to include the Eastern Stars, especially sister Yolanda Hands who held the dinners down and was the glue by which the two fraternal bodies broke bread weekly. We became family to one another and I quickly learned that the "military family" was that much closer overseas. It literally made the time go by faster in my opinion; it gave me plenty to do off the job in a positive way by giving back to the local community.

On October 12, 1997, my wife gave birth to my one and only son, Sean P. Hoggs II. As I sat in my dorm room waiting for my phone to ring for my mother-in-law to give me the news on the birth of my child, my fraternity brothers (equally as anxious) sat there with me. I tried to play it cool, but I just couldn't. I simply sat there on pins and needles. When the phone finally rang, Tonya's mother was on the other end; she said, "congratulations Sean, you have a son."

I was so overtaken by my emotions and so proud to be a father of a son, the tears streamed down my face. My fraternity brothers told me to get it together jokingly and unbeknownst to me, they had "it's a boy" cigars already on hand; it was a great "cherry on top" for the night. When I finally got to speak with my wife, I told her how proud I was of her and that I wanted her to get some rest. My entire lodge would soon cram into my dorm room and we would head out into the night to celebrate. We were truly like family; my joys were their joys. As my year in Korea came to an end, I had made some life-long friends. The bonds that were forged on the peninsula of South Korea will never be broken.

Departing Korea, aside from my son being born, two significant things happened. The first, one of the members of my Masonic lodge drowned in an accident falling into a "Binjo" ditch (where the rain water would run off so as to not flood the streets during the rainy season). The force of the drainage was incredible. We as GI's were always warned by the safety section to stay away from the Binjo ditches during the rainy season because a man or woman could be easily killed by slipping into one.

McAdams, the young man killed, had become like a little brother to me; we spent countless hours together and I welcomed him to the Masonic body as the master of the lodge. The day prior to his death, we had just had lunch together and we talked about life and both our futures, as I was getting ready to return to the states. Upon hearing about his death, I immediately spoke to his parents. His father, a Prince Hall Freemason himself, was proud that his son was initiated into the Prince Hall order prior to his untimely death. I called for Brother McAdams' Masonic regalia (gloves and apron) and had it sent home to his parents immediately. I shared a lot of time with this young man and I took his death very hard; he had a very bright future. We held a Masonic memorial service locally for him and I called for a "Lodge of Sorrow" for 30 days in his honor. Brother McAdams, may you continue to rest in peace.

Lastly, before leaving South Korea, I got called up to the squadron by my commander. Not sure of the inquiry, I knew that I had done my job to the best of my ability. To be honest, I thought that my commander just wanted to sit me down before I left Korea to give me the pros and cons of the work that I had done while stationed there.

Now walking into the squadron front door, the First Sergeant (the enlisted member who was the commanders' right-hand man or woman) was there waiting for me; I thought, this can't be good! As we walked in, he said that the commander wanted me to take a seat outside of his office. I sat there anxiously, doing a mental recall of everything that had transpired that year but I kept coming up with blanks. Up to that point, I had not gotten into any trouble; in fact, I spent the year mainly doing charitable work and raising money for scholarships for the local high school students (this is where I began to give back to man).

When the commander stepped out of his office, I immediately rose to my feet. Expecting the worst, I stood in complete silence and kept my eyes locked forward. As he approached me, he told me to stand at ease as he extended his hand. Mentally I did a big "whew," thinking the worst inside; I did not want to be put on administrative hold (which would have prevented me from leaving Korea and seeing my family and son). He said "Sean let's step into my conference room." When we walked into the conference room, the First Sergeant was there once again calling the room to attention; however, the commander was behind me so I was trying to figure out who was in the conference room and why were they calling the room to attention.

Upon entering the office, there stood the base commander along with my flight leadership and my flight mates. I was told to come to the head of the table and to stand next to the General. Still puzzled, I did not say a word as no one had yet told me why we were all there. The General said "Sean I'm here to personally inform you that you have been selected as the Pacific Air Force Commanders Logistics Plans and Programs Professional of the Year." I was dumbfounded, as I had no idea that I was even nominated for the award because no one said a word about the nomination to me.

I was so proud in that moment; there I stood with the base commander, a "One Star" Brigadier General. I was immediately humbled. My Supervisor Master Sergeant M. Knehans told me that my efforts in support of the readiness of the base had not gone unnoticed and that I warranted this award, designated by the Pacific Air Force Commander. Being a new Non-Commissioned Officer (NCO) (now a Staff Sergeant), I felt that I had truly arrived as a Jr. NCO. I would depart Korea shortly thereafter.

While stationed in South Korea, I was selected for my follow-on assignment back to the states; it would be to none other than McGuire Air Force Base, New Jersey (the 305th Air Mobility Wing, Logistics Plans Flight). I would be returning home for duty (just 45 minutes or so from Plainfield) after the many years of being stationed away. Tonya and I were very excited when we got the news of my next duty assignment. I knew that I had grown and matured enough not to be lured into the streets that once enamored me.

Truth be told, had I been stationed in New Jersey upon initially graduating from Air Force basic training in 1988, I would have been kicked out. I didn't have the maturity that I needed at the time and the allure of the streets would have drawn me back in without question. The Lord works in mysterious ways and he knew what he was doing at the time by sending me far away to K.I. Sawyer Air Force Base, Michigan for my first assignment, the "Winter Wonderland."

Chapter 15

Home Sweet Home, 9/11

Now stationed at McGuire Air Force Base, I worked as a part of the 305th Air Mobility Wing, Wing Staff. My Office worked directly for the Brigadier General in charge of the base and we were responsible for the mobilization and deployment of Wing personnel and equipment to meet Headquarters Air Mobility Command directives when called upon. After getting the family situated on base in our new home (the family no longer a stranger to moving in the military), I turned my attention to learning the nuances of my new job.

While I got settled into my job, I was also meeting my neighbors who lived around me. One particular neighbor, Ron Taylor, lived directly behind me. Before actually meeting Ron, I would always see him pull up in his white Honda Accord that was decked out with all the trimmings. There was nothing unusual about that, but what was unusual is that he would literally pull his car into his parking spot and take parts of his car apart every day. To this day, I still do not know what he was doing.

Tonya and I would actually joke around when he pulled in and say, "There he goes again tearing that car apart." On top of that, he would always put it back together that same day no matter how long it took him. I finally went up to him one day and jokingly said, "man that's a beautiful car, but you are going to tear it up taking it apart and putting it back together every day." He laughed and said, "nah, I know what I'm doing." We would become best of friends after that.

While the months passed by at my new duty station, I found that inner voice once again compelling me to do more with my life. As with Korea (as I was experiencing an innate paradigm shift in the way that I viewed my contributions to humanity), I was gaining a burning desire inside to help others. I felt a profound sense of guilt gripping me from years past for many of the transgressions of my youth dealt to me by the streets, ignorance, and circumstance; simply put, I needed to make amends for the wrongs choices I had made (now fully understanding the gravity of it all and that I did have a choice).

I found myself at the local YMCA in Plainfield, feeding the homeless month after month with other local organizations. I began to mentor young inner city males that shared my troubled background, explaining to them that life was not always fair but that they had choices. I participated in Operation Stand Down, an effort put forth to feed the many homeless military veterans in the greater Philadelphia and surrounding areas. Ultimately, I immersed myself in becoming a devout humanitarian and I would never look back.

Now a Non-Commissioned Officer and stationed in New Jersey, I owed it to myself and others to return to my high school where my first brushes of the military were experienced in JROTC with Lieutenant Colonel Rubel. I needed to share my story with the cadets of the program. After scheduling my visit, the day came when I was finally going to address the students in the Plainfield JROTC program. Lieutenant Colonel Rubel no longer worked at the school, but I was introduced to the new staff by the school principal that greeted me. Going back to my high school as a United States Air Force Airmen, and no longer that troubled youth, I was able to walk the halls this time with my head held high.

Meeting with the cadets, I was able to share my story with them; many were able to relate to the part of town that I was from and acknowledged the struggles that come from that part of town (I could see it in their eyes). I told the cadets that life was about choices, some good, some bad, and that the choices that they made now could have far reaching implications. I told them that I was no angel growing up (by any stretch), but that I was able to turn my life around for the better by ultimately understanding that the streets would be my demise. I would continue to visit my high school throughout my military career and many schools like it wherever I was stationed at throughout the world.

I began to stress the importance of an education whenever I spoke publicly; however, I was armed with everything but my own formal secondary education. Ironically, it would be my neighbor Ron (the Honda Accord owner) that would set the wheels of education in motion.

One day after speaking with Ron about life, opportunities, and future goals (yes, while he had his car in pieces once again), Ron literally said, "Sean, let's go back to school!" I said, "I'm in Ron, but if we start this, we're going to finish our degree," he agreed. And that simple, we were ready to begin college, this time with the resolve to finish.

Throughout all my years in the military up to that point, the one thing that ate at my conscience continuously was the fact that I had let Mr. Jeremiah Dix from Kean College down. He gave me an opportunity to attend college, one that could have easily gone to a more deserving student in the EEO program, and I let him and me down. This time I swore that I would finish school and make right (to a degree) what I had done wrong so many years ago.

School would start off slowly for Ron and me, taking a course here and there. But one thing was becoming very apparent—my gift for books never left me. At first I thought it was a fluke receiving an "A" here or there, but it became to be the norm of my classes. I became insatiable for school; I was now a mature and focused student. I actually enjoyed class and I looked forward to class debates on various topics whenever I was called upon in class. The military had served one of its many purposes in my life, instilling in me the discipline to stay the course regarding school.

Also fueling my passion for school was the fact that I had earned enough credits to get my Community College of the Air Force Associates Degree in Logistical Science. It had come to pass that the degree that was first introduced to me by my Air Force recruiter (as a selling point) was now tangibly within sight. I was so proud of this fact and I could not wait for the actual degree to be conferred. I was also thankful that Ron, my neighbor, had gone back to college with me as we pushed each other hard to stay the course. During this same time, I was diving deeper and deeper into community service with the help of Senior Master Sergeant (SMSgt) Karen Lamphere. Any free time that I had outside of my family time, I found myself giving back to the local community in one way or another. So, who was SMSgt Karen Lamphere?

Karen Lamphere was a "tough as nails" Senior Non-Commissioned Officer that demanded the best out of her troops. Unlike SMSgt D. from Pope Air Force Base from years back, she would serve as the example of what a Senior Non-Commissioned Officer should be like (in my humble opinion); she was respected by all (officers and enlisted alike) across the base. She was from Highland Park, New Jersey and she had the toughness to boast, easily taking one to the "wood shed" if warranted. However, in the same breath, she could be the sweetest of ladies (bringing in cupcakes for everyone's birthdays).

SMSgt Lamphere taught me everything about being an NCO outside of a formal classroom. She was a boss and had become my mentor and a mother-like figure to me. She understood my upbringing and she would lend me an ear whenever I needed one, and place her boot up my backside if I messed up; I respected her tremendously. She told me that I needed to embrace the Air Force's "whole person" concept, which was being involved and volunteering in the military community as well as the local community. Although I was deeply entrenched in community service already, I added the base piece to my efforts, taking part in base activities.

Under SMSgt Lamphere's guidance and tutelage, I would be named Team McGuire Air Force base Non-Commissioned Officer of the year for Jr. NCO's, that is, the top Junior Non-Commissioned Officer for the base. Once again I was humbled. In addition to receiving the award, I was also selected as the top graduate for the Community College of the Air Force Associate degree conferring commencement ceremony for McGuire Air Force Base. I indeed felt blessed, and I knew had it not been for SMSgt Karen Lamphere, none of this would have happened. Mentoring is a powerful instrument.

In a separate ceremony that year, I would be recognized by the USO, garnering the General George Van Clean Military leadership award for that year. I would rub elbows with the social elite for the first time in my life, most notably Mayor David Dinkins of New York City. My wife and I were also treated to a stay in the Plaza Hotel that evening; it was a far cry from years back of sleeping in cars and homes with no heat, lights, or water. Thank you for seeing something in me and believing in me Karen!

Valiant Carter or "Val," who was somewhat new to my Flight, was from Rahway, NJ. And although we were the same age, Val would become one of the biggest mentors in my life. Val was new to the logistics career field, and needed to "learn the ropes" regarding the COMPES system. At this point in my career, there was nothing that I couldn't do with the computer system, so I had in essence become SSgt Nate Middleton from K.I. Sawyer from years back. Val, a very driven and focused individual, became like a sponge, picking up all of the tricks of the trade. It was as if I was looking in a mirror as Val began to truly understand the computer system.

We spent a lot of time together while he learned the business of logistics; we naturally bonded over our shared background of the mean streets of Central New Jersey. Val was also pursuing his bachelor's degree at the same time while working at the Wing. Although I had every intention of finishing my bachelor's degree, as agreed upon by Ron and me, Val put it into a perspective that would forever cement my educational pursuit.

Sitting in our cubicles, Val said "Sean, you are articulate, you handle yourself well under pressure, everyone counts on your expertise to get the job done, but it all means nothing!" Stunned by his statement, (again him being my peer and same age), and me saying inside to myself, "who are you to say this to me?" I asked Val what are you talking about? He said "Sean, I'm going to put it to you bluntly, you need to get a bachelors degree and stop looking like and sounding the part of a formally educated man!" He was right.

Before I searched for a school that I could go to in pursuit of my bachelor's degree, I got a notice in the mail from my Junior College. When I opened the letter it said that I was selected for induction into the Phi Theta Kappa International Honor Society, Chi Iota Chapter. I had to read it twice because my name and "honor society" just didn't go together! I could not believe what I was reading. Phi Theta Kappa was literally one of the largest honor societies in the world, and here was the Bastard Child at its doorstep being invited in. It truly was becoming the case with me that I was starting to understand that education was truly the great enabler.

During the induction ceremony, I was so proud to be a part of the ceremony. Standing there with my Phi Theta Kappa candle in hand and shawl wrapped around my shoulders, I remember being overtaken with emotion. I could not believe where I was standing; it was a long way removed from the hustle and two senior years of high school. Proceeding to the stage, I remember an individual that I had been in class with a few times having a complete look of utter shock on her face when I walked passed her sitting in the audience. She could not believe what she was seeing. She asked me, "what are you doing up there" and I said, "Do not ask me what I'm doing up here, ask yourself what are you doing sitting in the audience!" I couldn't believe what she had just said to me. I had worked hard to arrive at this educational milestone, nothing was a given for me, ever!

Unlike high school, as I pursued my education in Jr. College, I was no longer a troubled student. However, because I was somewhat reserved in class (still a loner of sorts from dealing with the years of abuse from my childhood mentally), I only offered up my opinion on a given subject when I was called upon in class (eagerly willing inside). The classmate assumed that I was not collegiate honor material. However, I was focused on my education and I had my eyes clearly set on the objective. I was all too happy to disappoint her.

After working at the 305th Air Mobility Wing now for a few years, I found out that I would be reassigned to the 421st Ground Combat Squadron on Fort Dix, NJ (home of the "Black Hats," the symbol of the elite military trainer). As a result of finishing my Associates of Applied Science Degree, Headquarters Air Mobility Command (Logistics) selected me for instructor duty for a new type of training for logistics planners called Phoenix Readiness. I would be charged with building cutting-edge training from the ground up and implementing it command-wide along with Master Sergeant Bernard Palmer. At that same time, I also enrolled in the Workforce Education and Development bachelors' degree program at Southern Illinois University-Carbondale, via their satellite campus on McGuire Air Force Base. Ron would sign up for the program too, staying true to our pact.

After I had the logistics piece of the Phoenix Readiness program fully operational, I became even more focused on my off-duty education. I began to fulfill all of the requirements of my degree program and my bachelor's degree was becoming well in sight.

As I approached the completion of my degree, the Superintendent of the 421st Ground Combat Readiness Squadron, Chief Master Sergeant Gary Kelly, called me into his office. He said, "Sean I have only done this but a few times in my career, and that I am compelled to do it now." I sat there not knowing what I had done, or what to expect; the highest ranking enlisted member of my unit had called me onto the carpet, a place that no Non-Commissioned Officer wanted to be. He looked me dead in my eyes and said, "Sean it is time for you to leave the enlisted corps and join the officer ranks." I could hear the sincerity in his voice, but I just did not see myself as officer material.

The "Chief" went into great detail; he had my military performance records up to that point laid out in front of him (discarding my initial supply reports). He said that it was clear that I had earned the right to apply to Officer Training School (OTS). To me, it was unfathomable; I didn't come from the upper crust of

America or a privileged background. I was the Bastard Child from the streets of Central Jersey just trying to make my way in life, and besides, who was I to walk amongst the officer corps? Chief Kelly said that it was not up for discussion, and that I was to take the necessary steps to apply for OTS. He wanted a status update weekly for each requirement fulfilled.

I would be promoted that same year to Technical Sergeant (E-6). After passing the Officer Qualification Test (which was like the SAT test on steroids), and applying for Officer Training School, I was released from duty to finish my last semester of college under the Air Force Boot Strap program, a program utilized to complete your college degree.

By September 11, 2001, I was back on active duty. I was teaching in class when an announcement was made over the loud speaker to have all of the Phoenix Readiness Instructors report to the command section. There we learned that the Twin Towers in New York City had been attacked and that we were now on alert. In the days to come, we would send our military students back to their home stations and the Phoenix Readiness Instructors would be assigned to the main base as sentries for the security check points; it made for a trying time as everyone was naturally on edge. However, by this time I had a profound love of country and sense of duty; like many in the military, I wanted to meet our nation's enemy and threat head on! I would have to wait.

Initially, I augmented the Security Forces as a checkpoint sentry on McGuire Air Force Base after the initial attack on the towers. However, Headquarters Air Mobility Command would eventually reassign me back to my old unit under the 305th Air Mobility Wing as an "R" prefixed war planner from a specialized school that I attended years back called The Contingency War Planner's Course. I would serve as the COMPES Non-Commissioned Officer in Charge for the 305th Air Mobility Wing as they began to work missions to deploy personnel and assets to meet our nation's enemy head on.

In the months to come, I would work with the Federal Emergency Crews that were rotating in and out of Ground Zero in New York City. I got to see first-hand our nation's first responders respond to a nation in need; I was so proud to be an American. Needing a few more courses to complete my degree from the local Jr. College (transparent to the Boot Strap Program previously mentioned for the university requirements), I was literally going to school seven days a week while simultaneously supporting the war effort. It was a small price to pay in comparison to the emergency crews that were transiting through the base working around the clock at times, removing debris with their bare hands, bucket by bucket while looking for survivors. I would do everything in my power to get them whatever they needed as they sat and waited for military airlifts to return home. I simply viewed them as heroes, each and every one of them!

Prior to being temporarily reassigned to the 305ᵗʰ Air Mobility Wing, I was notified that I was selected for Officer Training School. My commander had informed me during a squadron commander's call after I was ordered to return home from a conference that I was attending. Chief Kelly was in attendance and he was the first person I thanked. To put it bluntly, I just could not believe it! I thought it was a joke or a mistake, and that my commander had someone else's paper work.

The Bastard Child, an officer . . . who would have believed it? NOT ME!!! It validated that with education, hard work, and dedication, the Air Force will give you an opportunity regardless of race, creed, religion, or in my case, socioeconomic background. It was a far cry from the good 'ole boy club that I experienced when I first joined the Air Force years back. I even found my way on to the national game show *The Weakest Link* during this time, making it all the way to the finals only to lose by not knowing the composition of baking soda. Regardless, I had a good time. My competitor won by answering a question regarding the age requirement to become the President of the United States; I was like, really? Versus the composition of baking soda . . . But things were looking up across the board. I wanted to do my part to combat the rising terrorist threat. They had attacked my home, my backyard in New York City, a place I knew all too well growing up.

I was notified by my Functional Manager, the authority that was going to tell me where I would be stationed at in the world as an officer, of my duty station options. I would either be stationed at the 352ⁿᵈ Special Operations Group in Mildenhall, England or the 353ʳᵈ Special Operations Group in Okinawa, Japan—both components of the Air Force Special Operations Command. My Functional Manager made it clear that those were my only two choices as a "prior enlisted officer" and to make a selection accordingly; I was given 48 hours to return my decision before one was made for me.

After consulting with the family, we decided that the 353rd Special Operations Group would be my assignment of choice. I would be working directly with the First of the First Special Forces Group (Green Berets), the 320th Special Tactics Squadron (Combat Controllers and Pararescue troops), along with the 17th Special Operations Squadron and the 1st Special Operations Squadron in pursuit of our nations Tier-One Targets. I was going to get to meet the enemy (al Qaeda) head on in the Pacific Theatre. However, before any of this could transpire, I needed to do one important thing, complete Officer Training School!

Chapter 16

Life Behind Bars

In October of 2002, I would enter the gates of Maxwell Air Force Base (Montgomery, Alabama) home of the Air Force Officer Training School; my wife would actually walk in my place to receive my degree in Workforce Education and Development from Southern Illinois University-Carbondale. Unlike enlisted basic training in 1988, there was no Military Training Instructor waiting for me when I got off of the bus; I was greeted by an upper-class officer trainee upon departing the bus and told to head towards the in-processing building. Not knowing what to expect, I followed everyone else as we found ourselves heading towards the building.

I walked into the building with everyone else, but it was surreal; I was entering an institution that created the Air Force commissioned leaders of tomorrow. I kept thinking about all of the officers that I had worked for under their command and I felt like I honestly did not belong there. Most of these "Officer Trainees" were from the upper crust of society. I did not have the pedigree that they had and secretly I was a mess inside, terrified; but I maintained my poker face as I navigated day one of Officer Training School (OTS). I also noticed that there were not too many faces that looked like mine and mentally it weighed on me. I knew I could not fail, I knew I could not go back; I knew I could not come this far in life and quit!

Upon meeting my Flight mates for OTS, it was a mix of prior enlisted members and non-prior enlisted members. There were 13 in all, and all appeared to be razor sharp, that is, except for me as I was still thinking *what am I doing here?* When we were assigned sleeping quarters, I was taken aback. The room actually looked like a college dorm room. There were only two twin beds to a room and wall-to-wall carpet, unlike enlisted basic training and the bay-style sleeping arrangements (26 to a bay). We had a private bathroom with two individual desks per room. I thought to myself, after having been enlisted for 14 years, *this is not going to be that bad.* However, I would soon discover that unlike enlisted basic training, (where everything is first taught by the Military Training Instructor), everything in OTS would be completed by the Officer Trainee by "reading the manual."

OTS was 13 weeks long and the first 6 weeks would be spent as an underclassmen, (of course the upperclassmen never let you forget that). Everything about OTS was very different from my enlisted basic training. Even the meals and where we ate was different. Not that the enlisted food was bad, trust me, but the dining area was a 180 from what I had previously experienced. There was a lot of emphasis on the academic aspect of OTS because the Air Force wanted critical thinkers, coupled with the ability to lead. We marched and did drill, but it was not to the degree of enlisted basic training where you marched every day. If there was one thing that matched the intensity of enlisted basic training it was the physical training aspect of OTS. Yes, one must have had been in shape for OTS or you were out the door.

A week away from becoming an upperclassman, it was time for the cadet or officer trainee wing leadership to rotate out. Knowing that I would not be considered for a position, I didn't trouble myself with the politics of it all. However, we were all required to interview with the squadron commissioned staff (all OTS candidates) regarding leadership positions as an upperclassman. Major Proctor, the commander, called the entire squadron into the training hallway after the interviews were completed and weighed by the commissioned staff. He said, "we have made a decision on the new cadet squadron commander that will work hand-in-hand with the commissioned staff, and it is Officer Trainee Sean Hoggs!" Thinking that I had a better chance at hitting the lottery, I was the last person expecting to have my name called. Literally I said to myself . . . "what!"

Now a Cadet Lieutenant Colonel, due in part to my years of being prior enlisted, I was at the helm of the cadet squadron. Yes, immediately the pressure was on. I had the responsibility of now running the entire cadet squadron for both the upper class and lower class cadets (upon their arrival). Anything that went wrong fell squarely on my shoulders. There was no room for error and I had to perform as required.

Surprisingly, the cadet squadron rallied behind me and completed every task on time that I asked them to complete. I had in some way earned the respect of my peers as an underclassman. I learned one very important lesson while I was in OTS: "you get more bees with honey!" I also was beginning to understand the thought process of an officer and how to navigate the shark-filled waters of the "A-Type" personality. Yes, OTS did indeed prepare you to be a leader. I knew then that true strength lay within one's mind and not one's fists!

Unlike enlisted basic training, OTS had a formal dinner with mess dress attire associated with it (formal dinner wear). Everything about

OTS was about leadership and intellect; in fact, my Flight class average was 97.7%. It was the only time in my life that scoring anything under a 90 on a test was unacceptable. It was extremely competitive at OTS and the Air Force made it that way. I made it my business not to slack in any aspect of Officer Training School. As the weeks passed by, I really began to understand the privilege and honor of being selected to OTS was. I owed it to so many that put me in this position to graduate, but more importantly, I owed it to my family and myself.

Graduation time came and I was ready to go. My Aunt Cynthia (a fixture in my adult life) was there along with my wife and some of my 421 Cadre members and my officer-in-charge who had flown down to support me. I could not believe the day had come for graduation. I would lead the squadron formation as its cadet commander with saber in hand as we did our "pass-in-review" parade for the OTS leadership. Collectively, we took the Oath of Office (the same as General George Washington during the birth of our great nation) in support of the Constitution and the President of the United States and we were now fully commissioned officers.

I simply could not believe where I was standing and that the Bastard Child had humbly arrived at a new chapter in life. In fact, if you would have told me in 1988 when I first enlisted into the military that I would obtain a commission in the United States Air Force, I would have requested that you got a drug test immediately! Education had once again enabled me to reach a place that I once thought was impossible.

This commission also belonged to those who had come from the same inner city environment that I had come from across this vast nation. It was a testament that we too can be somebody in America besides the thug or hood that so many of us are wrongly viewed as. It showed that we simply need one thing, a chance!

I thought back to my first officer encounter at enlisted basic training in 1988 and just staring at him in awe, as I now stood as he did years back. I literally stood in the mirror of my hotel room for about an hour looking at my "gold bars," my commissioning had truly come to pass. I knew from that point forward I would live my life as an officer, living "behind the bars" of a commission, appointed by the President of The United States. Tonya even chuckled at me as I stood in the mirror. To say that she was proud would be an understatement.

After all, she had been faithfully by my side since age 12; this commissioning was as much hers as it was mine.

Before leaving OTS, I had garnered the "Top Spartan Award" for my squadron. The award went to the number one Officer Trainee that exemplified the meaning of teamwork, leadership, and officer-ship. This award meant so much to me because it was not expected, but even more so because the award was an award that was bestowed upon me by my peers at OTS. I came to find out later, they had unanimously voted me as Top Spartan, and they alone were responsible for me receiving this award; the commissioned staff played no part in the selection, except for the presenting of the award at our final squadron "all call."

I was truly humbled once again in my life and at a loss for words; I didn't expect to receive such an honor. Here stood a man that was given nothing in life accepted by our nation's best and brightest as a leader amongst leaders. They had no idea what I had gone through in life (not wanting to use it as a crutch), and to receive this award from them was truly moving. It made me want to go to inner city America (any hood, ghetto, block, project, or set) and say: yes we can if we try (those that share my common thread). If you fall trying, get back up!

Now briefly back at the 421st Ground Combat Squadron as Second Lieutenant Hoggs, it was time to pack up the family and head to Okinawa, Japan. Before departing, the Black Hats would place my name on their wall of honor with the other Black Hats that had moved on. I will forever be in their debt for the skills that were taught to me by an elite group of specialized warriors.

With the 421st behind me, Special Operations would be my new home and I would spend the next two out of three years deployed as we pursued our nations Tier One targets in the Pacific Theatre (Yes, there was another pursuit of terrorists outside of Iraq and Afghanistan).

The day I departed for Okinawa, Japan with my family, my good friend Terrance Harris, (Al Pierre) would pass away that same day. I was on "must move" orders, which meant that I had to depart the U.S. May you rest in peace my old friend, for you truly had a heart of gold.

Chapter 17

Special Operations—A Call To Duty

Now on the island of Okinawa, Japan with my family and assigned to the 353rd Special Operations (Spec Ops) Group or "SOG," I was working side-by-side with America's most elite troops. I would cut my teeth fast, as this unit did not make allowances for anything short of precision-type execution. The SOG was good with a storied history and they knew it. I was fortunate in a few ways upon arriving to the Spec Ops unit. First, I would be working with an old friend from Pope Air Force Base in Technical Sergeant B. Trice. Next, the senior enlisted member of the Flight was from the Brooklyn, NY and razor sharp, Chief Master Sergeant K. Gordon. Rounding out the crew were what would turn out to be two of the best logisticians I ever had the pleasure of serving and deploying with—Technical Sergeant "J.T." Pryor and Major Rich Macalino.

I would deploy in support of the 1st of the 1st Special Forces Group (Green Berets), in pursuit of Tier-One targets that threaten our nation and our way of life (many of the missions, if not all, were classified). I also now understood that the war on terror truly spanned the globe, initially believing that the war would only be fought in Iraq or Afghanistan. This tour would serve as my front line battleground against the terrorist threat that resided in the Pacific Area of Responsibility. I would stand in some very far off lands while assigned to Spec Op.

I was proud to be assigned to the 353rd SOG and knew that it was a privilege to be allowed to serve in such an elite unit. I would learn so much about the Spec Ops way of life. In fact, I literally had to learn how to do my job all over again as many of the missions that deployed were Ad Hoc (that is, fast developed and fast deployed). It was far removed from the methodical planning that I had done as a logistician in the past. To look into the eyes of these elite warriors, you could see that they were "locked on" and ready to bring our nations' might down upon our nation's enemy. I had known many hard-rocks from the streets of Central Jersey (i.e., had a tight knuckle game, my brother Darrow included) and many of which would have made exceptional troops, but these men were different; they were experts, professionals at killing.

Strangely enough, to sit in an aircraft with these elite troops while being transported by the 17th Special Operations Squadron or the 1st Special Operations Squadron in pursuit of identified targets, I found they were comedians at times, full of jokes and pranks that they would play on one another. They would repeatedly clean and functions check their weapons in preparation of a mission, and I would soon learn to follow suit.

It would take me some time to acclimate to the destructive business as a Spec Ops troop, but slowly my mind locked onto the Spec Op way of life; even learning the deadly art of hand-to-hand combat from a fellow 353rd SOG member and former UFC fighter, S. Daugherty (a master at his craft). Along with the Green Berets, I also worked with the Air Force's version of its special forces, the 320th Special Tactics Squadron (which consisted of the Air Force's elite Para Rescue and Combat Controller teams). This was definitely a far cry from what was known as "Blue Air Force."

While deploying throughout the Pacific Theatre, I began to understand what poverty was like on an entirely different scale, a third world level scale, which was simply hard to imagine, unless you were able to witness it firsthand. Shanty Towns became all too familiar to me. I would come to see and understand world hunger on an entirely different level as I would walk the far off lands and witness third world poverty first hand. Having grown up and having had to make my own way by my own hand as an early teen, I was in no position to call into question the trials of my struggles as a young man anymore, after witnessing the unimaginable poverty abroad.

In many of these countries, the children would panhandle and ask for money from the "GI's." American military personnel with their big hearts, me included, would reach deep into our pockets and give whatever we had in hopes of the young children getting some food. However, it would be the case in some countries that these children would use the money for other things besides feeding themselves. It is a cruel world out there and one can only imagine where the money would go-to. "Huffing" or "sniffing glue" by children was very evident in some of the countries that I deployed to. You would see the glue in their little hands (street kids), and they would hug it close to their body like a mother would hug a newborn child.

To watch these children meticulously "huff" this coveted glue— poison—made me cringe each and every time I would lay eyes on it. They would crack the lids of their containers ever so slightly, and inhale the fumes, giving them the high that they craved so desperately.

I refused to give them any more money. These street kids would make a gesture towards their mouth with their hand to signify that they were hungry, saying "eat, eat." Initially I would give any money that I had, and or loose change to them, upon this gesture.

It would take the locals to explain to me that the money that I was giving to them, or the money that I would collect from the GI's to pass forward, would be used strictly for drugs. I wanted to contribute to their wellbeing but not by inadvertently buying them drugs. J.T. Pryor, who by that time was my constant wingman (enlisted partner) for deployments, would help me try to make a tiny difference in the lives of these unfortunate street kids across the scope of our deployed Area of Responsibility. As Mother Teresa once stated, "If you can't feed a hundred people, then feed just one." J.T. and I would come up with a strategy to ensure that any money raised would go towards the intended goal.

After deploying to a given country, and after setting up our deployed work area, we would collect funds from the GI's. First and foremost, we had to make sure that it was safe to go into the areas that we wanted to frequent. Once that was established by the appropriate authority, we would take the money that we collected from the GI's and go buy bags and bags of food, understanding that the American dollar was so much stronger than most of these countries' currencies, it allowed us to buy food in abundance.

Because we were logisticians, we were able to understand the lay of the land because we were utilizing local contractors to support the missions. It would allow us access to areas that would let us hand out food to the children. It came to pass that no matter where we went in the world, J.T. and I would find the local slums and make it our business to try and make a difference in the lives of these impoverished children. We both realized that we could not change the world, but we knew that we could make a difference in a little way. The children would come to know us as we would deploy to some of the same areas at times, and they knew we would come bearing gifts, food that is, by the arms-full. Their smiles spoke volumes.

Some of the missions that I deployed on were more dangerous than others (deployment exercises excluded). However, a very humbling thing started to occur while I was supporting these missions; my classmates from Plainfield high school, the class of 1986 to be precise, were beginning to reach out to me via email one-by-one. They were letting me know that I was not alone and that they were there for me if I needed someone to communicate with while I was deployed. They also kept me in their prayers (thankfully so) as I faced the reality of meeting our nations deadly threats a half world away.

Renee Sterling, "Dink" Matthews, Keith Bilal, Tyrell Scott (also a member of the U.S. Air Force) and Billy Wray would be constant figures in my life while I deployed in support of Special Operations. Some jokingly reminded me to get back safe to Plainfield so that we could enjoy a Fat Boy Cheeseburger from Red Towers, Black Cherry Soda (my favorite), and some house music (A staple in the city of Plainfield). I also owed the streets of Plainfield a huge bit of gratitude as my "streets smarts" were honed there through the "school of hard knocks" and I would employ them constantly while deploying throughout the Pacific Theatre in pursuit of our nation's Tier-One targets. Soon, all of my skills would be put to the test.

On Sunday, 26 December 2004, with an epicenter off the west coast of Sumatra, Indonesia, an earthquake struck with unprecedented power resulting in a devastating Tsunami that would forever change that region of the world. I got the call in the early hours of the morning just a few days removed from Christmas. The Special Operations Center or "SOC" of the 353rd Special Operations Group called an emergency meeting in which the leadership would spell out the SOG's role to play in the days ahead in support of the humanitarian relief effort. When the manning (troop selection) was determined, I was told that I would be deploying out with the initial chalks (sequenced movement) as part of the Advanced Echelon or "A-Team," as the Group Commander referred to it.

I kept a "Go-Bag" (a military travel bag packed with the essentials for an initial 30-day deployment) packed for moments just like these as part of Special Operations, I was set to go. I told my family that I was deploying in support of the Tsunami relief effort and that I did not know when I would be returning. I would soon find myself deploying on the back of a MC-130 Combat Talon II along with the SOG commander and mission essential personnel deploying to a classified location.

Once we landed, the operations began. The U.S. Forces set up what equipment they had. I would sit in the initial meetings with the command element and the host-nation representatives as we negotiated some real estate for the follow on forces still yet to come. Although we were in the country by their State Departments request, the atmosphere at the deployed location (especially at the negation table) was anything but receptive for us!

My commander spelled out his logistical needs to me and I was paired with a contracting officer. There were many items that would need to be procured by way of the local populous, but the local populous, like the host-nation representatives, were not eager to do business with the Americans. It made it almost impossible to get the base camp set up for full operations. In fact, we could not even procure a forklift to support our on loading and offloading operations, although I could see many throughout the deployed location. Our translator would always say that an item did not work per the owner, but Stevie Wonder could see that it was a lie. I would have to turn to the U.S. Embassy, by way of my Joint Task Force Commander, to have an operational forklift sent immediately to my location and additional equipment.

My first 72 hours on the ground, I literally did not sleep. It would be another 24 hours before a relief logistician officer (an Army Captain) would deploy in and take over responsibility as the ranking individual. The logistical decisions being made for the 353rd SOG up to that point, were levied strictly on me.

Lieutenant Colonel R. Samuels, the Operations Officer on site, would always refer to me as "Major Hoggs" while deployed there, jokingly he said I was performing at a pay grade two levels above my current rank. It was a humbling compliment, but truthfully I was getting worn down fast and it was taking its toll on me. I kept my game face on in front of the brass and the enlisted troops, but I was squarely on the ropes on the inside. To make matters even worse, I was trained in a strict Air Force discipline regarding logistics and the Marine Brigadier General would call for all daily situational reports to be in Joint Service language (that is, readable by all branches of the armed service and not just the Air Force). I would literally have to take out the Joint Doctrine manual and translate the day's business into a readable joint service message (a daunting task for the layman).

When the Army Captain did arrive, I welcomed him with open arms; he understood the different supply classes that were required to be reported on in "Joint Doctrine Language." In fact, I was so tired and in desperate need of sleep, that when I did finally get to get some rest, I apparently hung up on my Operations Officer (second in command) during a conversation we were having. Truth be told, I didn't even remembering him calling me. Yes, I was that tired!

Now with all of the assets in place, the follow on forces bedded down, and the supply chain established, I was able to really take in the devastation that the Tsunami had caused. I was literally at ground zero and the sights that I laid eyes on reminded me that nature was truly a destructive force when unleashed. I fully understood the amount of lives that were lost, the homes, and the hunger that was gripping that area and I made it my business (along with my troops) to do anything within my scope of power to bring relief to this devastated region; operations would run 24 hours, 7 days a week. Rumor had it that the news anchor Diane Sawyer had come through our site on her way to report on the Tsunami on board an MC-130.

I slept in my work area, although we had "Jersey barriers" surrounding the bed-down area. If looks could kill, you could see the hate for the U.S. in the eyes of many. My "gut" told me to sleep at my worksite for fear of terror bombings, so that is what I did, along with many of my troops. My work area was roughly a hundred yards from the established bed-down area. The food, although pleasing to the eyes, would be ravaged by the presence of roaches, and I mean all over the place. I stuck with a healthy diet of military Meals Ready to Eat, more commonly known as "MRE's" and bottled water. The weather was scorching hot and there was no shortage of the duty day. Everyone earned his or her stripes and bars on this deployment. Upon my commander's final return from the U.S. Embassy, I was given the order to prepare for redeployment. Once packed, we sequenced the forces out and returned to Okinawa, Japan in less than 48 hours.

It was a benchmark moment in my military career. I got to lead as an Air Force officer on the world stage, trusted by my superiors to do a monumental job that required a skill set well above my pay grade with U.S. assets totaling over 1.1 billion dollars. I had come a long way from my days in Plainfield, NJ and John Street; yet in part this success was as much theirs as it was mine. The toughness gained on those streets once again gave me the mental toughness to be resilient in the face of incredible pressure. There's no place like home.

I will never forget the devastation and human loss as long as I live. I would receive the Humanitarian Service Medal for my actions in support of the Tsunami relief effort by my superiors who trusted in me. I would also be named the 353rd Operational Support Squadron Company Grade Officer of The Year for 2004, a component of the 353rd Special Operations Group. Once again, in the presence of God, by way of his mercy and grace, I was humbled.

In between the multiple deployments while assigned to Spec Ops, I found myself back in school. I was ready to attempt what seemed to be the impossible, my Masters degree. I knew in order to be competitive for promotion to Major, eventually I would have to complete Squadron Officer School (SOS), an officer's first critical level of professional education and complete my graduate degree. Still a Second Lieutenant, I knew I was a few years away from attending SOS. However, as highly suggested to me by a number of "senior officers," I needed to complete my Master's degree before I put on Captain.

At the Captain rank, I would be becoming a "Flight Commander" where I would not have the luxury of time to complete a graduate degree, or if I did attempt it, it would be extremely difficult.

I took their advice and immediately began my graduate program at the University of Oklahoma by way of their overseas military program. You had to fulfill the same degree requirements as state side, there was no difference in the curriculum requirements and the professors emphasized that point repeatedly. The professors from OU's main campus were flown into the island to teach the various courses.

Although tough (because of constant short notice deployments), I would eventually complete my graduate degree. My nuclear family would be in attendance for the commencement ceremony and like high school, I would sit in disbelief. I just could not believe that I was in possession of a graduate degree from the University of Oklahoma. Again it was a far cry from sleeping in cars and hustling for my next meal back in New Jersey. I could no longer deny that life was full of limitless possibilities, even as the Bastard Child.

I was becoming "worldly." My views on life were starting to change; I was beginning to understand the world from a global perspective. Years removed from my childhood, I still could not escape the horrors of my childhood, still challenged subconsciously when I slept (yes, still waking up in a soaking bed from colds sweats). But awake, I was truly embracing what life was placing before me. My hurt and anger in life was beginning to turn to understanding and forgiveness. I really started to realize that I was blessed by God to be given the chance to live such an incredible life up to this point, despite the crosses that I had to bear.

My family by this time was well adjusted to the island of Okinawa, Japan and my youngest daughter even picked up the Japanese language. When we returned to the states, she would speak it fluently at Japanese restaurants and it would always catch the proprietors off guard when she would order for the entire family in Japanese. We even got used to the typhoons that were associated with that part of the world. In fact, we would all sleep in the living room together and "camp out" as we rode out the many typhoons over the three years while being stationed there. It was now time to depart the island and return to the states. I was more than ready having literally deployed for the most part of my tour while stationed on Okinawa, Japan.

Luck would have it that the 353rd SOG Commander was best friends' with the 816th Contingency Response Groups commander at McGuire Air Force Base, New Jersey. He asked me if I would like to go and work in the contingency operations world, and naturally I agreed; after all, it was home. Of course headquarters would have to approve my new assignment, but the SOG commander said that he would do everything in his power to see that I was considered for the job. It was at this point in my life that I realized that in life "it is not what you know, but who you know at times!" I eagerly awaited to hear back from the assignment personnel.

When the official notification final made its way to me, I was all too happy. I raced home that day and let the family know that we would be returning to New Jersey for my next assignment. The families on both sides were happy to hear of our return. Before leaving the island, I made sure to stop by my Group Commander's office to thank him for recommending me to his fellow commander for the assignment.

The family and house was all packed and ready to return to the states. Our last few nights on the island were spent in military lodging, and although it was a very comfortable room, we were ready to return home to the United States. Tonya and I would actually go to South Korea for a little shopping before leaving, but as a family we found our way to Hawaii for a much needed family vacation; Grand mom (on my wife's side) and my Aunt Cynthia would join us in Hawaii, and then Newark Airport in New Jersey would be our final destination.

Chapter 18

The Garden State & TOYA

Now back in the Garden State after a long flight, we were all too happy to be home. We would catch a shuttle van from the airport back to Plainfield (the van trip home seemed like 10 minutes after the marathon flight). It was good to see the Route 22 highway and the sights and sounds of New Jersey. I will always remain a city kid at heart. It had been a long three years and Special Operations had left an indelible print on my soul. Like many veterans, it would take me some time to get acclimated to being back in the states and the everyday business of life. Red Towers Diner (the local restaurant that I made mention of earlier regarding my classmates and where my parents initially met) would be our family's first guilty pleasure upon returning home. I would treat myself to that coveted Fat Boy hamburger with cheese with a large fry (with salt, pepper, and ketchup) and a large Black-Cherry soda. It was every bit of a *"Lord of The Flies"* around the fire moment for me; good to be back home— pure bliss!

Once I signed into my unit, I got my family situated into base housing on now "Joint Base McGuire-Dix's-Lakehurst," and no longer McGuire Air Force Base. Not much had changed since I departed except me; this time I would be a Flight Commander, a Captain, with all the responsibilities falling squarely on my ability to lead and execute the daily mission of the 816th Global Mobility Squadron Air Transport Flight, as directed per Headquarters Air Mobility Command. I was humbly confident and ready, as I was just coming off of the most demanding assignment of my military career in Special Operations. My troops were sharp and they responded well to my direction. I felt blessed to have the subordinates that were assigned to me. Each of them was a go-getter by their own right and we were all Devil Raiders (the unit nickname).

As time passed in the unit, an opportunity presented itself that I just could not let slip through the cracks. There was a military teaching vacancy at Rutgers University made aware to me by way of the Headquarters Air Force Personnel Center (a military advertising of a special duty assignment). If I applied, they would consider my application for the position. Excited, I spoke with my leadership and my career field manager to see if it was feasible for me to be released for the position at Rutgers University, and they both said yes.

The thought of me teaching at Rutgers University, the state university of New Jersey, seemed unimaginable to me. I remembered that Rutgers was the very first school to turn me down when I applied to college years back after my second go-around in high school as a senior (and rightfully so). I was an educational risk back then (Kean College was a testament to that). But this time, I was prepared; I had my "squares filled!"

After applying for the position (and Rutgers had to formally hire me for the position in writing), I was informed that I would be reassigned as the Commandant of Cadets for Detachment 485 at Rutgers University. My life had come full circle; the Bastard Child had gone from the obscurity of the streets to teaching at the state university of New Jersey. Education had once again opened a door that at first was unimaginable!

Before taking the permanent position at Rutgers, many significant things would happen in my life while assigned to the 816th Global Mobility Squadron. The first—I would return to Florida (the Altamonte Springs area) after being far removed from my time living with Amelia. I would return there by way of a military conference, the Tuskegee Airman, Incorporated conference. I was chosen to sit on a company grade officer discussion panel that addressed being a minority officer in the armed forces.

At this conference, it would be the first time that I got to rub elbows with those that I owed so much to, the original Tuskegee Airmen. Their storied history, coupled with their pride of service and love of country, was nothing short of awe inspiring at the conference. Had it not been for them and their incredible sacrifices, there would be no Captain Sean P. Hoggs. I tried to shake as many hands to offer up my thanks for leading the way to as many of these living legends as humanly possible.

One of my mentors at McGuire Air Force base (a fraternity and chapter brother of mine by way of Omega Psi Phi Fraternity, Incorporated) would turn out to be none other than an original Tuskegee Airman, Lieutenant Colonel Thomas H. Mayfield (the recipient of the Congressional Gold Medal, one of the highest honors in the United States). Before his passing, he would present a plaque to me (in his name) having served as the keynote speaker years later for a scholarship banquet in his honor; it would be the last time he would present a plaque to anyone, as he passed away shortly thereafter. I cherish the humbling gesture deeply to this day. I felt extremely privileged to be mentored by a national treasure and American hero. May you rest in peace Lieutenant Colonel Thomas H. Mayfield; your legacy will live on through those who continue to wear the uniform.

I had some time in-between meetings at the conference, so I took it upon myself to go and see my nieces of my deceased brother Jeff (after all I was too close not to make the effort), which would put me eye-to-eye with Amelia after all those years. However, this time I would not return to her as a scared little child, but as a man.

Strangely, I still remembered the address to Amelia's house (for me, a house of horrors). I placed the address in the GPS at the hotel and then proceeded to her home to find the whereabouts of my brother's children (not having any contact with them but knowing he had children). As I drove towards Amelia's, my mind raced with so many dark memories. With my brother no longer alive, I tried to think of the positive memories that we did share as siblings, but my mind kept flashing back to the brutality that I endured as a child. When I pulled up to the house, it was run down. Before going to the door to knock to see if someone was home, I collected myself like I was going on a mission that I knew would be a dangerous one. Mentally I was ready, my anger was under control, and I approached and knocked on the door.

Standing there waiting, it seemed like an eternity before the door slowly open. My mind raced with what was on the other side of the door. Was it that monster that tormented me? Was she still a massive woman as I remembered? Good, bad, or indifferent, I wanted to see my nieces and nothing would stop that. As the doorknob turned and the door opened, to my surprise there stood a very frail woman, much different than the woman I had come to know. I could tell it was Amelia by the one gold cap that greeted me in the airport so many years back when I was six years old. However, time had made her might and size but a mere hint of herself from years past.

Having left the conference in my uniform, I startled Amelia when she opened the door. She paused and asked, "Can I help you?" I sat there for a few seconds then said, "Amelia, it's me, Sean." It took her a minute to realize just who I was, then like a light bulb being turned on she said "Sean, oh my God, look how big you are!" She asked me if I was a police officer and I said no, and that I was in the Air Force as an officer; she immediately invited me into the house. Stepping through the threshold of the door, my mind (like the time before) kept flashing back to the first steps that I took into her house as a mere child.

Looking around the house sent chills up my spine. When Amelia sat down in the living room, I asked her if it was all right for me to walk around the house a little; she said "Yes!" The house seemed so much smaller now, almost gloomy, as if it carried a sad history to it as both Jeff's (my brother the Jr. and his father the Sr.) were now both deceased. The back room where I spent so much time by myself was like revisiting a jail cell for me. I slowly made my way around the rest of the house (alone this time). I searched my soul for understanding and peace before sitting down and talking to Amelia one-on-one at length.

I asked Amelia could she call my nieces, having never seen or talked to them, and tell them that their uncle from New Jersey was there to see them. She said to give her a minute while she tried to call one of them via their cellular phone. She then let me know that the oldest daughter had moved away, and that she doubted that she would be able to get a hold of the younger daughter. When she removed the phone from her ear, she said that she got a voicemail. I had to accept the disposition of the call attempt; my visit to her was unannounced, and she didn't know I was coming (ironically, she would not give me either one of their phone numbers when I asked). Disappointed, now knowing that I would not see or speak to either one of my nieces, it was time for me to finally confront a childhood demon face-to-face and to ask the simple question, why? Why the brutality? Why the mental abuse? Why such hate towards an innocent child?

Amelia started to tell me all about her life up to that point and I sat there in amazement. She really had forgotten (or had selective memory), about what I had experienced in that house by her hand. She actually had told me that she "made a mistake by letting me return to my mother years back and that she wish she would have kept me." Inside, I said . . . what! God again by his mercy and grace removed me from that situation, I'm sure my years growing up there would have resulted in pure unadulterated pain and terror.

Once Amelia got through talking, it was now time for me to exorcise my personal demon. I asked Amelia, "Do you remember what you put me through? Do you remember the vicious beatings that I suffered by your hand?" I told her that I remembered, vividly, and that for years I suffered mentally as she added to the brutality of my childhood. She sat there startled and then jokingly said that she meant business back then about discipline and that it was how she was going to teach "hers" to "mind" her! I looked at Amelia and said that her brand of punishment was exclusive to me only and wrong; I was a child! I asked her why the deep-rooted hate, but she acted as if she could not remember what she had done to me (or again had selective memory), but that she demanded to be "minded."

With my anger growing, incredibly calm overtook me suddenly; I realized at that moment that she had no more power over me. It was at that point that I accepted that she might not remember because of her old age (giving her the benefit of the doubt, selective memory aside). For me, I just wanted to look into the eyes of a monster that had enacted such hate and brutality towards me, and to let her know that what she had done to me so many years back had not broken my spirit, but ultimately fueled me and made me stronger as a person.

I told her that I forgave her, although it was clear that she was but a mere shadow of the intimidating person that I once knew; time had not been kind to her since my brother's death. My intent was to see my nieces, but to see Amelia one-on-one and to forgive her (in the end) did wonders for my soul. Forgiveness is truly a powerful instrument. I brought this chapter of my life to a close. I asked God to have mercy on her soul for the harm she levied against me.

Ironically, the only thing that she asked me before I left was could she have some money. I gave her the $40.00 or so dollars that I had in my pocket, hugged her (coupled with a kiss on the forehead), and wished her the best in her remaining years. I knew I would never return to that house again after saying goodbye. Amelia would pass away some years later. May she rest in peace and forgiveness!

After the conference, I returned back to New Jersey and I would never look back, knowing her power over me was no more.

That same year while living on Fort Dix, I received a letter at the house from Southern Illinois University-Carbondale (McGuire Air Force Base campus), the same program that I had graduated from years earlier. They were extending an invitation for me to be the commencement speaker for the graduating class of their military program on McGuire Air Force base; without hesitation, I humbly accepted.

After accepting the university's invite, I began to write the speech of my life up to that point. I owed so much to this higher institution of learning that had afforded me, and so many others like me in the military (spouses and dependents alike), a world-class education and a key to the world. To even remotely entertain declining the invitation was unfathomable to me. I was humbled by the opportunity.

The day of the commencement ceremony, the soon-to-be graduates lined up, eagerly awaiting to receive their diplomas, and rightfully so, as most were active duty personnel as I was years back, and I knew the sacrifices that they had made to get to this moment. I had my cap and gown on as they did (adorned with my Master's degree shawl from the University of Oklahoma). As I prepared to give my speech, I looked out into the crowd; every seat was filled.

Once again, I found myself far removed from my earlier days "on the block." The great equalizer (education) had taken me from the streets to the grandest of stages for a major university. Standing with the official party waiting to be introduced, I took a second to collect myself. Once the ceremony began, there was no turning back.

Being introduced by Dr. Westberry, I sat there briefly in amazement. I simply could not believe where I was at in that moment of time, and that in a few minutes I would be addressing the graduating students on behalf of Southern Illinois University-Carbondale. There were parents, husbands, wives, children, senior officers and senior non-commissioned officers throughout the audience. To say that I was nervously caught up in the moment would be an understatement. In my eyes, the impossible had happened; from my haunting past now stood a proud United States Air Force officer ready to give the speech of his life.

After my formal introduction, I made my way up to the podium. I took a sip of water and cleared my throat. As I began my speech, I thanked the graduating military members for their service and sacrifices to the nation. I told them that I understood what they had just accomplished in academia and that it was no easy task, given our nation's pursuit of the Global War on Terror at the time (as I mentally recalled working on school assignments while supporting the 9/11 missions years back). I told them to be proud of their station in life and that their loved ones and leaders in attendance were all proud of them.

Bringing my speech to a close (having addressed my main points), I shared a little bit about my life story with the graduates and audience. My point was a simple one regarding my life, that education is, and will always remain, the great equalizer in life! To that, I am a living testament. I reminded the graduates that "The sky's now the limit for you. Let your sails down and explore the world." I reminded them that their time had finally arrived as a graduate of this prestigious university with a storied history supporting the military around the world.

That same year, I would be asked to be the alumni speaker at my high school 20-year class reunion; I was again deeply humbled. I would dedicate my speech to the many men and women of our class, especially the mothers. I thanked the first responders (police, firefighters, EMT's and military veterans) that were a part of our class, having gained a tremendous amount of respect for them all as a result of working with the emergency crews from the 9/11 terrorist attacks in New York City and serving in the military. I also thanked Renee Sterling, Keith Bilal, Dink Matthews, William Wray and Tyrell Scott for their unwavering support and friendship that they provided to me while serving in Special Operations (there are simply no words that can capture my deep gratitude). The e-mail communication with them (while deployed) helped pass the time and briefly removed my mind from the dangers that I faced on many missions.

Shortly after serving as the university commencement speaker and my class speaker, unbeknownst to me, the most incredible thing to ever happen to me in my life was about to unfold, (outside of the birth of my children and my marriage).

Lieutenant Colonel S. Gericke, the 816th Global Mobility Squadron Commander, called me into his office. He sat me down and began to ask me about my life in detail; he said that he had read through all of my performance reports as an enlisted member and as an officer and thought that my journey in life up to this point was nothing short of "miraculous," given the odds that I faced growing up (based off of previous conversations about my life). He would always say that I was the most driven company grade officer that he ever had work for him.

My commander was a very upfront and honest man, and I could tell that he was truly intrigued with my life story (up to this point I didn't know why). As I served as a flight commander underneath him, I made it my business to "deliver the mail" for him each and every time my flight was called upon to execute the mission. If there was a tasking from the Group (the larger unit associated with my squadron), he would always call on my duty section to execute the directive.

I had a fierce sense of loyalty to him because he had a genuine concern for not just me, but all of his troops; learning in life that you take care of those who take care of you! He would even call my number to take part in the planning portion of the historic first-ever bi-lateral military exercise between Russia and the United States; I would go as the lead logistician for the 621st Contingency Response Wing, (now as a Captain).

The U.S. delegation would stay at a hotel located right outside of Red Square. The bulk of our days would be spent negotiating the hardware and forces that the United States wanted to bring into Russia and what Russia would allow the U.S. to bring in. It was obvious that our weapon systems were far superior to theirs and they knew it, so Russia would push back on anything that would make them look inferior in the eyes of the world and to the U.S. Ultimately, the exercise was cancelled because the Russians did not want to be up-staged by the U.S., but it made for an incredible experience for a kid from the inner city streets of New Jersey, (never in a million years would I ever imagine standing in Red Square). I was extremely humbled that my leadership had the trust and confidence in me to negotiate the logistical aspect of this attempted historic joint venture on behalf of the United States.

I have to admit that the Russians and State Department rolled out the red carpet for the United States while we were there. The incredible sights (to include seeing the original KGB headquarters) will forever remain ingrained in my memory; coupled with the fact that I did not see another black face the entire time I was in Russia outside of the U.S. Forces.

Riding their subway made for a unique experience (putting it mildly). I felt like a celebrity as many of the citizens stopped me to take a picture with them. I guess there were not too many black people in Russia. But, for all I had learned about Russia, (taking the Cold War into account), their citizens were very warm and embracing towards Americans.

I tried some Russian delicacies, but I found myself eating at the McDonalds right outside of Red Square for breakfast and dinner while I was there on business, passing on lunch completely. After trying the local cuisine when I first got to Russia (where cow tongue was served daily with their meals), I'll just say at night I became very friendly with the plumbing of Russia.

Once I returned from Russia, my commander had finished gathering his information about me. He told me that there was something that he was going to do with all the information he gathered, but that he could not tell me right then and there. In my mind I knew him to be a very stand-up officer (one of the best), but I was at a loss regarding his intentions. I inquired into the nature of his research, and he said "Sean, despite your station in life now, you have overcome some incredible odds to be where you are in life today." I thanked him, but his answer was somewhat elusive to me, but I trusted in his actions because he had my complete trust (something that I didn't give away too easy given my life).

A few weeks later, he would call me back into his office. He said that he wanted to let me know about the nature of gathering all of my information together, as well and sitting me down to find out more about my background. He would go on to tell me that he had the blessing of the 621st Contingency Response Wing Commander in his actions, as he planned to move forward with his intentions.

Naturally, I wanted to know what was going on. My commander said, "Sean, despite the incredible odds you've beaten in life, you have managed to give so much back to not only those around you but to the world." He said that he would have never known what I did outside of the unit had he not read my previous reports from past commanders (which led him to sit me down and begin a conversation about my life a little). He knew I had stayed active in the community locally, but had no idea what I had done across the globe until he read my reports. I've always made it a habit not to talk about my charitable deeds, as I believe that they should always come from the heart.

My commander said that he wanted to submit me for the "TOYA" award. I said what in the world is a "TOYA" award? He said, "Sean, it is an acronym for the Ten Outstanding Young Americans award." I still had no clue what it all meant. He would go on to say that in his 20 plus years in the military, he had never come across an extraordinary set of circumstance like mine that warrants a TOYA submission. I took him at his word, but he told me to go home and to really do the homework and understand the legacy of the award and then come back to him once that was done.

So, as he suggested, I went home and began to search the Internet regarding the Ten Outstanding Young American's Award. As I began to read, I soon realized the magnitude of the TOYA award, and that it was considered one of the oldest and most prestigious awards that the nation would bestow upon an individual going back to the early 1900's. Its past alumni literally contained the who's who of our nation! I remember thinking to myself that there was no way that I belong amongst them. That list included the likes of Presidents, Vice Presidents, Senators, and American icons, to include: John F. Kennedy, Gerald Ford, Bill Clinton, Richard Cheney, Nelson Rockefeller, Orson Wells, and the list goes on. The name Sean Hoggs just seemed a little out of place amongst them to say the least.

After doing my research, I went back to my commander and asked him was he sure about submitting me for a TOYA award. He chuckled and said, "Sean, I have a strong feeling about this and I am going to move forward on the submission." That said, I provided him with whatever he requested but deep down inside (after understanding the legacy of the previous TOYA winners), I thought he was really wasting his time!

After my commander was done with my submission package, I never followed up on the status of the nomination. To put it mildly, I thought it was a valiant attempt at him saying *good job Sean for turning your life around and helping a few others along the way*. Like I stated earlier, my commander was a very stand-up man, so I knew he meant well, but I literally thought that my chances were slim and none at being named a TOYA. I went back to doing my everyday job as a Flight commander, executing the mission as a part of the 621st Contingency Response Wing.

Shortly before reporting to Rutgers University to begin my teaching assignment, I was called into my commander's office. Having not spoken a word about the TOYA submission, I thought that my commander wanted to talk shop. So, as I had in the past, I grabbed my pen and pad and made my way to my commanders' office. He sat there stone-faced when I entered; I waited for his direction regarding the meeting.

He said, "Sean, do you remember when I submitted you for the TOYA award?" And I said, "Yes" . . . He said, "Well I'm happy to inform you that you are a semi-finalist for the TOYA award and that I have your press release information that you must fill out in case you are selected as a finalist." At that precise moment, I thought he was speaking some foreign intergalactic language to me. I simply could not believe what my ears were hearing! His face then lit up with a huge smile and he said to me, "Sean, sometimes you have to believe!"

When I went home that night, I shared the news with my family. I told my wife what an incredible honor to be a semi-finalist was and that I was happy to get that far. Initially I never told anyone, to include my wife, about the award submission because I really thought that it was unattainable for me. I was at a loss for words. Of course my wife and kids were extremely proud of me, but Tonya got a little upset because I didn't share the initial news of the submission with her. I explained to her that I didn't share the news with her because of the chances that I thought I really had no chance given my research on the award. I offered up my small apology and we moved on from there.

In the weeks to follow, it seemed like my unit leadership was on edge in a good way. It almost became religious in my unit as I was asked daily had I heard anything yet from the TOYA. My answer always remained the same, "I think my TOYA run is over." I was just happy to have been selected as a semi-finalist. The Lord had blessed me with so much by this point that I could not deny his divine favor, despite what I had endured in life.

Word would finally come down by way of my squadron commander. Befitting, because he was the one who really saw something regarding my life that he believed warranted a TOYA submission. He did not bring me into his office to notify me, nor was I called into the wing commander's office. Instead, I noticed a gathering of officers and enlisted troops right outside my office door; something was up!

It fast became standing room only in my duty section; naturally I asked what was going on. When I stepped out of my office, I soon realized that the entire floor was packed wall-to-wall. My commander, swimming through the crowd, made his way to me. He said, "Sean, I'm here to inform you that you have been selected as one of the Ten Outstanding Young American's for 2007." Based on the crowd and the senior leadership throughout the room, I knew that this was not a joke. My life would forever change after that moment.

The first thing I did was give thanks to the Almighty God above. While my leadership and fellow members in arms came up to congratulate me, all I could think about was life and how incredible it was. How did a beaten, battered, and homeless child (my time in the shelter) who survived the mean streets of Central Jersey, who lived in an abandon home with no lights, water, or heat as a teenager (not knowing where my next meal would come from at times) end up amongst America's elite as a TOYA recipient? Many gave me absolutely no chance in life, and now I stood with the likes of Presidents, Senators, and the who's who of American society. To say that I was humbled would be a serious understatement.

Shortly thereafter, the press began to start calling. I would do interview after interview by telephone for magazines or in person for the newspapers. It appeared that everyone but me knew about what a TOYA was. I truly had no idea regarding the amount of attention that this award would garner until I was announced as an actual TOYA selectee. However, my first order of business was to thank my squadron commander for submitting me and seeing something in me that I simply thought was not indicative of a submission. Never in a million years would I think that my life and my small contributions to man would ever place me amongst such distinguished notables.

When the particulars began to unfold, I was informed that I would have to attend the TOYA award recipient's dinner. The black-tie awards ceremony would be held in Omaha, Nebraska on September 22, 2007. It was said of my TOYA class in the press release that, "If history can be our judge, we may find tomorrow's most prominent businesspeople and politicians among the 2007 Ten Outstanding Young Americans honored this year." After reading the press release, I immediately wanted to know who the extraordinary inductees of my TOYA class were; because I did not feel worthy of this humble honor. Outside of me, I knew whoever else was selected as a TOYA that year was a serious "mover and shaker" on the national stage (in order for the press to make a statement of such), but who were the other selectees?

In time, my fellow inductees would be disclosed by way of correspondence from the TOYA selection committee. I began to know them one-by-one over the time leading up to the black-tie affair; they were all very impressive in their own right. To note, one started an organization that improved the quality of life for children with HIV/ AIDS; another was a microbiologist that was a premier scientist in the discovery of medical countermeasure against lethal diseases such as the Ebola virus, SARS, and smallpox. Another was a doctor who was published after discovering new insights regarding various blinding diseases. And last, just to name a few, was an individual that had won an ESPN Espy award for the Best Athlete with a disability and was a bestselling author. All of them were extraordinary individuals.

Next to them, I tried to put my contributions towards this world into perspective. Did I live up to the Ten Outstanding Young American Jaycee Creed: "That earth's great treasure lies in human personality, and that service to humanity is the best work of life?" Of the categories to be considered for a TOYA award, I would find out that I was submitted under the "Humanitarian and/or Voluntary Leadership" category. The work I had done feeding the homeless around the world (in large part with J.T. Pryor) and the U.S., coupled with the mentoring and volunteer work across the globe, would ultimately earn me a TOYA selection.

I never thought anything like this would happen to me, as helping people across the planet was done strictly from the heart. My commander would go on to tell me that, "Sean, I do not think you really understand how much good you have done in this world." I again humbly thanked him, but inside I was saying to myself that I hope that my small contributions to man, in some way, make amends for my transgressions of my youth.

Now in Omaha, Nebraska for the day of the event, and having met with the TOYA representatives, it was time for each TOYA recipient to give their speech. Before doing so, we would be treated to a closed-door reception and we would be introduced to the who's who that was in attendance. Everything surrounding the event was exceptional, from the hotel accommodations, to the meals; no level of detail was left subject to chance.

Prior to giving the speech, as a TOYA class, we were taken into the ballroom where we would each give our respective speeches later. To say that I was overwhelmed would be putting it mildly. The ballroom was extremely elegant, yet huge! I remember thinking to myself, there are going to be a lot of people in here. As I mentioned before, I had given a few speeches by this time in my life, but nothing to this magnitude! The presenter's stage alone looked like a page taken straight from Hollywood and the Oscars. Elvis Presley, who was also a TOYA recipient during his life, once said that although he had performed on many stages, that the TOYA stage had him terrified and nervous given the magnitude of the award. Now, if Elvis Presley was rocky, it was safe to say that I was a complete nervous wreck, a "soup sandwich."

After the TOYA recipient's reception, each TOYA winner was given a large box filled with the programs for the night's event. At first I didn't understand what was going on, but it was explained to us that we were to autograph every program in the box on our corresponding biography page; these programs were going to be sent to the various "VIPs throughout the country." I thought who in the world would want my autograph? But they were very serious about it and made sure that every book in the box was signed. At that point, it really began to sink in that I was joining a very exclusive fraternity unlike any other in our nation.

It was now time for the formal dinner and the speeches to begin. We were kept in the reception area until we were called for; I became more and more nervous by the minute. My mind raced with all kinds of questions: was my speech good enough? Did I really belong there? What if I messed up with my family, commander, and all those people in the audience? Yes, I was feeling every bit of what Elvis Presley must have been going through. When the time finally came for us to join the banquet, we were escorted into the ballroom; a sea of people rose to their feet with a thunderous applaud. This was a far cry from my days in the streets and the shelter.

While each TOYA recipient gave their respective speech, I remember thinking to myself that these are truly Americas best and brightest; their stories were simply amazing as they unfolded before me on the screen and through their words, they were all phenomenal and compassionate human beings. I again felt that I did not belong to be mentioned in the same breath as they did. As each speaker finished, it meant that I was that much closer to stepping on that stage.

Finally, the moment of truth was now at hand; my introduction was my cue to make my way to the platform like we had practiced earlier that day. Watching my life story unfold on the screen as I approached the stage was surreal. The TOYA committee had captured my life story and contributions to the world and made a remarkable video (to see it was incredibly humbling, it put things into context for me). At that precise moment, for the first time, having my life put in context before me, and my contributions to man highlighted, I felt that I humbly belonged amongst the other winners.

With each step I took towards the platform, my heart began to pound harder and harder, as if it would burst through my shirt. Now center stage and looking out into the crowd, I realized just how many people were in the audience from a "birds-eye-view." Before saying a word, I collected myself; I knew this would be the speech of my life. I took a deep breath and I prepared to give my speech, prepared weeks before. You could hear a pin drop it was so quiet before I said a single word, or at least that was what I was thinking.

When I began to speak, I thanked the panel of judges who selected me for this tremendous honor. Next, I thanked my family that was in attendance and my squadron and wing commander. And last but not least, I thanked my Lord and Savior, Jesus Christ. My speech painted a picture of my life, from my humble beginnings as a child, through my troubled years as a teenager and then my time in the military. I expressed that day on the stage that life, no matter how difficult, was to be embraced, explaining that someone, somewhere on this earth had it harder than you.

I explained to the audience how I would find myself feeding the homeless in my hometown when no one knew. How I wanted to make amends for many of the wrongs that I had done as a young man in the streets of New Jersey. I explained that I got to know poverty firsthand by life and by traveling the world while in the military, trying to make a difference with my bare hands, at times carrying food to those in need. That life was not about receiving, but giving back to humanity with everything you had. How education propelled me in life, and how it leveled the playing field for me.

I acknowledged my fellow TOYA recipients that night on stage; I applauded them for their contributions that they had made to this great nation and the world. It was clear that we all shared a burning desire to do one thing, make a positive difference in this world, whether it was in medicine, philanthropy, or for humanity. For a moment that night, I thought back to Chris my Resident Assistant at Kean College who was the first one to say, *young man trade in your baggy pants and hoodie for slacks and a dress shirt, and be somebody.* At that moment, I realized he was saying "Sean, it's time to be a man and not a statistic."

Standing before that crowd, I knew that my life had come full circle. It was amazing and I could proudly look out into the audience knowing that my life's work as a humanitarian had made a difference in some small way. I understood what the TOYA's were acknowledging, but the award that was placed in my hands at the conclusion of my speech was not mine, not by far; it belonged to everyone who had helped me along the way to get me to this moment in life, for they truly deserved the credit, to include those who abused me. I had taken that abuse and channeled it towards positive momentum.

When I went to exit the stage, I noticed the audience began to stand and applaud. First it was just a few people, then a table or two, then the room in its entirety. They kept their applause going; it's as if no one wanted to sit down. Even making my way back to my table, my wife said "Sean they are still applauding!" I could not believe my eyes or ears as the cheers continued; I was humbly brought to tears. Looking back on my life, I knew at that point that I wouldn't trade it for anything in the world, despite the physical brutality that I endured and the psychological scars that I was still dealing with. What was supposed to break me in life had only made me compassionately stronger. Faith—in a person's belief, ability, or purpose—is an incredible thing.

At the conclusion of the formal ceremony, each TOYA recipient was escorted to their own personal autograph signing suite. Not thinking that I would be autographing many programs, I told my wife Tonya that it would be okay if she came into the signing room with me. I set her a chair up next to mine at the table that had been set up for me. With the door closed, I had a few minutes to collect myself, but again I didn't think that there would be anyone outside of my door that would want an autograph, a few at best. I told the TOYA representative that was assigned to me to open the door, again reminding my wife that we would not be there too long. To my surprise, when the door to my suite was opened, there was a line of TOYA attendees waiting for an autograph.

I was overwhelmed by the response that was standing before me. The line literally stretched from my autograph table (the back of the room), out the door and all the way down the hall. I could not believe what was happening. Tonya looked at me and said "this is incredible." She had been a part of my life since I was 14 years old and had seen my life (our life) come full circle, culminating in this moment. As each person came up to me, they were expressing how moved they were about my life story and speech, and how I should put my life to paper in an autobiography because it is a story that must be shared. But at the time, a book seemed inconceivable. I would actually receive an email months later after the TOYA awards from an official asking me if I had started that book yet because America needed to hear my story.

As the night continued, the line was not going down. To my surprise, everyone waited for an autograph. I was humbled by everyone who came up to me to share their heartfelt thoughts. I signed as many autographs as humanly possible, and I was proud to do so. It was a magical night, a once-in-a-lifetime moment, and I knew that America (regarding the opportunities to rise above a given station in life) had opened her arms up to the Bastard Child—a child born with a heavy cross to bear in life, but also of hope, resiliency, and perseverance. My pedigree was not of the social elite, but of the mean streets of inner-city America. It was a testament that it is not where you start at in life, but what you do with your life while here on this earth. From that point forward, I knew that I could look anyone in the eyes and say that nothing in life is impossible, but first you have to believe. This is when I adopted the saying, "results, not excuses in life!" If I could go back in time, I would tell so many of my friends caught up in the hustle, that there is another option no matter how dire the situation is. Not that everyone should go into the military, but that they should at least finish high school and give education a chance to enable their opportunities regarding their future, for I am them.

Chapter 19

Trouble in Paradise

Now at Rutgers University, my office gave me an incredible birds-eye-view of "College Ave;" it was paradise for me. I was now an Associate Professor at the school that I so desperately wanted to attend years back, but was unable to (by my own effort, or lack thereof in high school). The weather was somewhat still nice when I first arrived at Rutgers. I remember taking a walk down College Avenue to take it all in. I went down to the student cafeteria and I just sat there and took in the sights and sounds of college life as an Associate Professor, barely touching my meal.

Rutgers, its students, and faculty, were very friendly; everyone seemed to speak no matter where I went; who says New Jersey people are rude? I even made my way to the teachers' lounge a few times for lunch; I wanted to test the waters as a new professor. Yes, I found it all hard to believe. I even made a stop at the infamous "grease trucks" on College Ave that the students cherished so much to try out some of the local delicacies.

My students were sharp as cadets (and the regular students who just took my class). I could tell that every one of them brought something to the table and that all of them were extremely intelligent. I kept a poker face on at all times as the Commandant of Cadets, but in the classroom, I let my hair down just a little as an Associate Professor of Aerospace Science. Believing that in order for a student to learn, there has to be a permissive learning environment. The students seemed to respond well to my teaching approach. I have to admit that I wanted to stay on top of my game because I was extremely proud to be teaching at such a prestigious university (understanding the true history of Rutgers University).

By this point in my life, I had been a mentor to many people throughout the world. I felt I was tailored-made for my new job. I would get to know many of the cadets very well and I would get to hear about each of their life stories. Some were from very privileged families, while others had worked their way up to this point in life (some prior enlisted military). I tried to impart as much wisdom to the cadets, and the "real world" Air Force before they commissioned and moved on. If a cadet found him or herself in a predicament, I always tried to walk them through the thought process that would help them remedy the situation.

Like with anything in life, there were some times at Rutgers that brought about tough situations for some of the cadets. Any time a cadet had to be removed from the program for one reason or another, I took it personally. They were all great kids, but with life, as with me in my youth, sometimes they make bad decisions and, as a result of those decisions, some would have to be turned away from the Air Force, or commission. You could see the passion in their eyes because they simply just wanted to serve their country, but repeated lapses in judgment ultimately became their deciding factor and exit from the program.

There were no shortages of young Americans stepping up to the ROTC program at Rutgers and it was a welcomed sight! My cadet staff rivaled any unit that I had been a part of. They were sharp and they completed any task that I put before them. They simply made my job that much easier at Rutgers; I had their trust and they had mine. It was impressive to see what Rutgers and the Air Force had put in place. The cadre at the detachment was second to none. It seemed that this is where I was born to be (the classroom). I simply loved the job, Rutgers University, the mentoring aspect of it, and more important creating Air Force officers. It couldn't get any better than this!

Hitting on what felt like "all cylinders" at Rutgers, in October of 2008 my life would take a dramatic turn. I was very active in Brazilian Jiu Jitsu at the time and I thought that I had pulled my calf during training. Not thinking too much about it, I rubbed my calf down with some sports cream and I tried to continue on with life. However, the more I sat at my desk at work, the harder and harder it became for me to get up and simply walk around. I would carry on in this fashion for a few days until I had to go see a doctor.

Now at the on-base clinic, the on-base doctor said that he wanted to have a few X-Rays completed on my left leg. He asked me was it hard for me to walk and by that time it was almost impossible for me to walk. In fact, at home for me to walk to the bathroom (which was five feet away) was becoming a monumental task. My leg felt like it was a thousand pounds. Once the X-Rays were confirmed, I was told that I may have a blood clot in my left calf and that I needed to go to the hospital right away, so that I did.

At the hospital with Tonya, they read the diagnosis from the base physician; they immediately brought in an ultrasound specialist to take a look at my leg. The specialist confirmed that I had a Deep Vein Thrombosis (DVT) in my leg. While he tried to explain it all to me, I kept asking myself, why me? The doctor said that I would be discharged but that I would have to take Lovinox injections (blood thinner medicine) into my stomach in order to break up the DVT in my leg. I would also have a nurse that would be stopping by the house to check up on me daily. Easy enough I thought, not knowing just how serious this all was.

The first day or so at home I had no real issues. I sat primarily on the Lazy Boy chair in my house, with limited movement and my leg propped up like the physician directed. Like clockwork I took the injections as directed, not missing a single dose! However, my leg continued to ache and grow in size as well as harden to the touch. Sitting in the living room, my wife had just come back from grocery shopping. She asked me if I needed anything while she started to prepare dinner; I remember the food smelling so good.

With dinner complete, my wife had brought my dinner plate over to me but suddenly I had no appetite. Still sitting in the Lazy Boy, I felt a pop in the lower left portion of my chest; it was as if a balloon had burst and the air was leaving it ever so slowly. My body soon slumped over to the left, and I was desperately gasping for air. I could see all around me, but it was as if I was not in my body anymore. My wife immediately noticed and asked if I was all right. I could barely speak, let alone breathe and my situation was going from bad to worse. My wife dropped her plate on the floor and said that we were going to the hospital right now (her fast thinking most likely saved my life).

I barely had any clothes on and I fought my way to the floor to slip on something that my wife had brought down stairs for me to wear with her help. I could no longer walk. I actually crawled to the car with my wife's help. We both believed time was of the essence regarding my life, we didn't want to leave it to chance to have the ambulance come and pick me up, and it was two towns over. After fighting to get into the car with each breath, it was all I could do to sit back. I knew something was horrible wrong, but what?

My wife made her way through traffic with the hazards on, only slowing down to work her way through the red lights. Once we made it to the hospital my wife Tonya pulled right up to the entrance and ran inside for help. Within a few short minutes I saw the wheelchair being pushed up to the car. When I went inside I was moved up as an immediate priority. Since they had just seen me days before they knew the nature of my situation once Tonya gave them my information. I was then taken into the back and awaited treatment.

While in the triage area, Tonya was sitting next to me. We could hear the discussion that the doctors were having about a patient who they believed was not going to make it through the night; they said they were going to make them as comfortable as possible but they were not expecting a good outcome. I looked at Tonya and said, "Let's say a prayer for whoever that individual is," because I know they have a family and loved ones, it may be his or her last day on earth. When we bowed our heads we heard the words "stat," which meant that they needed to move on this patient right away, but we continued to pray. I told Tonya, "Thank God that I made it to the hospital or that could have easily have been me," while I fought to breath.

Right as we were done praying, the doctors and nurses came rushing into my room. They had briskly moved Tonya away from me and began cutting my clothes off. "That person" that they were talking about was yours truly, me! I could not believe what was happening. I was laid out on the gurney and immediately the IV tube was entered into my flesh, blood was being drawn, oxygen was being administered, and I was told not to move at all. In my mind I was screaming, "what in the world is going on?" And more important, by overhearing the doctors, I knew I was given less than 24 hours to live.

I was thinking, is this really my last day on earth? The Bastard Child was finally going to pay the ultimate price with his life. I had fought so hard to overcome it all, just to die like this. I didn't get it . . . I wasn't ready to die! My personal faith was being put to the test!

My heparin drip was set up immediately to try and combat the clotting. I would find out that I had suffered a Pulmonary Embolism (PE); in fact, I had suffered multiple PE's at the same time. The mortality rate for just one pulmonary embolism was 50% and I had multiple (PE's). Understanding that, I knew why the doctors had given me zero to no chance of surviving the night, but to their credit they kept fighting. I was placed in the Critical Care Unit, which was one above the Intensive Care Unit in regards to patient care. I could tell that they did not expect me to live through the night although they were fighting hard to keep me alive.

They set a chair up by my bedside for Tonya; she would stay there anchored, to the point that she actually got bed sores on her buttocks by the time it was all over, needing medical attention herself because of it, refusing to leave my side for a single second. She thought that if she left, I would die! She was literally trying to "will me" to live. I could barely breathe, taking tiny breaths. I had to fight and breathe on my own to stay alive. I was told that if they put a breathing machine on me that it could move the clots that were in me, thus causing my death. I sat there unable to talk or move and I began to really reflect on my life.

I began to question why my life had to be so difficult. Why did I have to fight for everything, even the simplest things in life, like breathing? Why was I always the object of someone's anger, rage, or hate? Believing that I only had but a few hours left on this earth, I asked God to forgive me for all of my transgressions (sins). I looked at Tonya and knew that she would be a widow and my son and daughters would be without a father. Tears ran down my eyes and Tonya would wipe them away slowly as she fought back her tears, putting her head down so that I would not see her face at times as she wept. The hours darkened and I simply felt life slipping away from me. I prayed that I had made amends for my days in the hustle by becoming a devote humanitarian, and accepting Christ as my Lord and Savior (asking for forgiveness). I desperately wanted to see my children one last time to tell them all that I loved them dearly, but I didn't want them to see me in the condition that I was in. I wanted their memories to be good and lasting memories, not of me on my deathbed. As the nurses checked on me continuously, I felt it was a dying cause.

At about 3 AM, I knew I was about to take my last few breaths. I looked at Tonya and with every ounce of strength that I had in my body I whispered to her that I loved her and the children and that it was time for me to say goodbye. I simply could not fight anymore. As I slipped away, I remember coming back in and out of consciousness as my heart fought to keep me alive. My memories were like snap shots of that moment. At first there was just Tonya and me in the room, then regaining consciousness (my heart refusing to give in) there were nurses in the room and Tonya had been taken out of the room, and the third time I regained consciousness the doctors were in the room fighting to keep me alive.

I was given a series of shots that would bring my breathing down to a shallow, but I guess the doctors wanted me to initially build up the strength on my own before giving me the shots; I really had no choice because the ventilator machine was not an option as previously mentioned. I was stable, but the pain I endured is simply indescribable; it was like having a knife violently stuck into my heart and lungs every time I took a breath. I would survive the night although I slipped away initially; *maybe God is not done with me yet,* I remember thinking.

I knew at that point what God wanted me to do, why he left me on this earth. Having initially refused to share my life story on paper, it was clear that God had given me my life and the experiences to share with others. To show that nothing in life is impossible, despite being weighed down with such a heavy cross to bear in life. To eliminate the excuses for those who were looking for them in their life to say why they could not do it. To show that "Joe nobody" could become somebody (however big or small) with hard work.

I now understood in that moment why I was asked to share my life story at the TOYA awards. I understood now that the life story was mine, but the message is for someone else, someone that feels like life is impossible. It was about saying it could be done. When the doctor stood over me the next morning, he said, "It is a miracle that you are alive!" He said by all accounts in his experience, no one had ever suffered as many PE's simultaneously as I did and lived to tell about it. I told him (now able to speak slightly) that God was not finished with me yet, and that I now had something to do by his hand. The doctor pointed out that by me not drinking or smoking, (I gave drinking up years earlier and I never smoked) and staying in shape helped in saving my own life. Luckily, my heart stayed strong throughout the entire ordeal.

Although I had made it through the night, I was by no means "out of the woods." I would stay in the hospital for seven more days as my body began to cannibalize itself as it fought to stay alive. In just seven days, I had gone from a solid 220 pounds to 160 pounds. My bicep muscle was so small that I could fit it in-between my index finger and thumb. I was not in a good place at all. My fraternity brothers (of

Omega Psi Phi Fraternity, Incorporated) would come and spend time with me from the moment visiting hours began, until they would have to be put out at visiting closing hours, "Friendship is Essential to the Soul." They made sure that my wife was taken care of and that my children did not want for anything. Additionally, many of my students at Rutgers reached out daily to check on me. Sitting in that bed, I knew that I had to fight on, even as the PE's were taking a toll on my body.

Over time, I became strong enough to be discharged from the hospital. However, I was but a mere shell of my former self in just a week's time. When I departed the hospital, I would be wheeled out in a wheelchair; I was only able to take but so many steps on my own. I would have to learn to walk again, first with a walker, then crutches, then a cane and finally on my own. I was told that I lost the full use of my left leg permanently and that I would have to wear compression socks for the rest of my life (to keep the blood circulation inside my left leg). For an athletic guy it was the kiss of death!

The one thing that probably saved my life (staying in shape) would no longer be an option for me. I would remain incapacitated and out of work for six months while my body tried to rebuild itself. In addition, the military would put me on a permanent profile, which limited my deployment status; my world was beginning to crumble all around me. Again, I asked why . . .

Sitting at home for six months recovering, I wanted to know one simple answer, how did this happen? I didn't drink or smoke and I worked out literally five days a week, to include Jiu Jitsu. Garnered from result of the medical test, it was discovered that I had a genetic blood disorder and that my blood, at some point in my life, was going to clot up. It was not a matter of if it would happen, but when it would happen. I think that all of the time that I spent on the back of the MC-130 aircraft in Special Operations played a big part in serving as a catalyst for the injury. It was then explained to me that I would be on blood thinners (Coumadin) for the rest of my life. When I was informed about my ailment and Coumadin, I actually chuckled. The doctor looked at me strangely and asked was I okay, as I laughed. I told the doctor that this was "par for the course" regarding my life.

While recovering, I would deal with a serious bout of depression; the "Ego," the "Super Ego," and the "Id" where all at odds with one another. The military man in me kept saying, "Suck it up," while the other aspects of my psyche were in a complete state of shambles. To look into the mirror (weak and frail), I would just break down, while simultaneously asking myself angrily, "What are you crying for Sean? Man up!" My painful past, coupled with this traumatic event in my life were collectively catching up to me; that "final straw" was at hand. I literally wanted to end it all. I looked to the painkillers that I had been prescribed to be my way out. I was done with this life; I was tired of getting the snot kicked out of me. Again, I kept asking myself what I did in a past life to deserve all of this. No one should have to go through this; the emotional rollercoaster was simply incredible. It seemed like every time my life had some type of normalcy to it, chaos would once again usher itself in.

Luckily, as the time passed and the pain killers decreased in dosage, the less I thought about ending it all, realizing that it would be the single most selfish thing in the world to do. To rob my children of their father, my wife of a husband, and my friends of our bonds—it would be the ultimate act of betrayal. Suicide would be the easy way out, and nothing up to that point in my life had been easy, so why cop out now? I thank God that my depression was only temporary. I began to think about that moment on my deathbed when I realized that I did have a greater purpose in life in accordance with God. To share my story with the world, or those that needed to hear it. I began to really focus on getting better so that I could return to Rutgers. I was fully removed from my temporary bout of depression and suicidal thoughts brought on by the Pulmonary Embolism. I missed the students and I wanted to get back to some type of normalcy in my life. Although it would be a long and tough road back, I would return to Rutgers University April of 2009, a half a year later.

Still very frail and weak, I made my way back to work, but still walking with a cane. All of the students were there to greet me at the detachment that day. I was very humbled by their gesture and it let me know that I did belong at Rutgers University and the "RU" family. I would pick up the pieces where my life left off at and I would get back to the business of being an Associate Professor. However, in keeping my promise to God and myself, I began to do the research for my autobiography. It was a painful experience, at times revisiting the many demons of my past, but a journey that I had to take; as I humbly suggest, that someone out there in my similar situation in life, needed to know that it could be done, even against incredible odds. They needed to know that anything is possible in life if you just try.

I was no millionaire by far, but I was comfortable and had made an honest living in life, without having to look over my shoulder. I was no saint, yet I tried to make a positive impact in this world. Ironically, the echoes were growing stronger and stronger to put my life to paper and to share my story from all around me (friends, family, colleagues and those that I had mentored). Even my students at Rutgers after a while began to nudge me on to write my autobiography. It is as if the world was saying, "Sean, it is a must . . ."

Time began to wind down at Rutgers University and my return back to the regular Air Force was at hand. I would find out that I would be reassigned to the United States Air Force Expeditionary Center (where I was a member of the 421st Ground Combat Readiness School, Black Hat unit). I welcomed returning to the unit; I still had many friends there. It was ironic that where I would become an officer, I would retire as an officer, a part of the same unit.

I would be selected for promotion to the Rank of Major, a Field Grade or senior officer while reassigned to the unit. What had simply seemed impossible was possible; I had gone from an E1 Airman Basic in 1988 to a Field Grade senior officer selectee 0-4. I point this out because it's been the premise of this book, *education put me in this position*; yes some luck and chance played a part, but none of it would have been possible without an education, *starting with the foundation, a high school diploma*. Looking back, I thank God that the events of my life returned me to high school for that second senior year. No one knows God's ultimate plan, but I am glad that he kept his grace on me even when I unknowingly took his grace for granted.

Before leaving, the cadet commander and the cadet corps of Detachment 485 presented me with a glass-encased Rutgers football jersey with the signatures of the entire cadet corps. It had never been done before regarding a departing Commandant of Cadets as far as I knew in the detachments history; I was speechless! Here stood a humbled man, who in a million years would have never dreamed that he would be an Associate Professor at Rutgers University, being presented with such a humbling gesture from its students. Once again, it reaffirmed that anything in life was possible. The gesture had let me know that I had made a positive impact on America's youth (what I was most proud of). I would even be extended an invite to guest lecturer at Oxford University in England as a result of being an Associate Professor at Rutgers University. From being homeless, to being sought after by Oxford University; again I say education is a powerful instrument!

To the cadets, cadre and administration of Rutgers University, the State University of New Jersey, I offer up my sincere thank you for the incredible impact that you have made on my life. After departing Rutgers University, many of the cadets, until this day, still keep in contact. Many of my underclassmen former cadets, upon their commissioning, invited me back to be their presiding commissioning officer, a humbling gesture that I cherish deeply.

Chapter 20

It's so Hard to say Goodbye

When I began my transition from Rutgers University to my final unit before I retired, I would befriend an earthly angel, someone who personified strength, resiliency, and faith. Her name was Kaiya. Our paths would cross because her mother and I were friends from high school and I knew that she was leading the effort to battle Cystic Fibrosis, a condition that was affecting Kaiya.

I asked her if it would be okay if I led an effort to seek donations through my fraternal organizations to raise funds. She agreed and naturally I wanted to meet Kaiya next. This was simply a cause that I could not walk away from; the humanitarian in me was immediately drawn to the effort. How could I go halfway around the world and help others and not help out one of Plainfield's very own?

After her mother was comfortable, she finally gave me permission to speak with Kaiya (after she was satisfied that my efforts were sincere). She was naturally protective and understandably so. By this time, Kaiya knew that someone in New Jersey was trying to raise donations for the cystic fibrosis foundation that was established for her and that she was going to speak with that person.

Kaiya lived in Florida at the time so the phone was our best means of communication versus e-mail or Facebook. When the time came, I finally made the call. Her mother had given me a designated time and I watched the clock like a hawk as the hour approached. As the phone rang, I listened to hear her voice on the other end. Like a scene right out of a movie, when she picked up the phone and spoke, she simply had me at "Hello!" It was literally the most angelic little voice that I had ever heard on the other end.

After our initial conversation, I asked Kaiya if it would be okay if we spoke every now and then (as I had done in the past with others that I had mentored, not that she was a mentee); she agreed. We would go on to establish a great friendship and bond. I would go and visit Kaiya in Florida from time-to-time and I enjoyed getting to really know her.

Kaiya spent a lot of time in the hospital and we would sit there for hours on end and play a ton of games as the doctors would come and go. She hated whenever I would beat her in a game, but the time we shared was simply priceless. However, make no mistake about it, she was a fierce competitor and hated to lose! She was also a humble diva in her own right and a beautiful young lady at the same time.

To note: If she was ever in any type of pain, she never showed it or complained while I was there. She took great pride in her appearance and she was always dressed to impress. Not one to make excuses, she lived life to the fullest every day; she actually had more energy than I did at times.

Kaiya and her spirit were strong and her resiliency was simply incredible. She had a strong relationship with God and we would talk about religion at times (her knowledge of the Bible was remarkable). I had known some pretty tough men in my life, between the mean streets of New Jersey and the military, but I did not know true resilient strength until I meet "Ms. Kai" as I called her.

Ms. Kai was a Dallas Cowboy fan and I would always give her a tough time about it jokingly, me being a Steelers fan. But as a testament to our friendship, I actually went out and purchased her a Tony Romo jersey (in pink) for Christmas. I told her that she must be really something special to get me to buy a Dallas Cowboy jersey. I'll never forget the hug that she gave me when she opened her gift up (squeezing the life out of me); that alone was priceless. Her smile could literally light up New York City. Her sincere passion for life made me realize that life is always to be embraced, regardless of the challenges or situation.

Watching her receive her medical treatment (breathing treatments and medication), she would just simply roll with the punches. I would always ask, "Are you okay?" And she would always say "Yes," then giggle with that cute unique laugh of hers. Funny, here I was a grown man, yet a young resilient girl was teaching me so much about life and living. I believe God crossed our paths for a specific reason and I am a much stronger person for having Kaiya touch my life.

I had given Kaiya a set of my captain bars that I had worn on my uniform. Her mother said that she would always wear them on some part of her outfit that she was wearing for that day or on her purse. If Kaiya did this to show that in some small humbling way that I had become a hero to her, little did she know that she had become my hero as well!

Kaiya would finally receive a lung transplant and she would live that much longer (she was a natural fighter). She would transition from this world to the heavenly realm and I would be devastated by the news. There is not a day that goes by that I do not think about her;

her battles put my battles in context for me. Not to question God's work, but I know he brought an angel back home to be with him. This world was graced by her short presence here on earth, but the lasting imprint and legacy that she left behind with so many will live on forever.

I am eternally grateful for having met such an angelic soul in my lifetime. In our short time together, she taught me so much about life. Kaiya would also be one of the voices that would encourage me to write my autobiography; she would always say that it is the right thing to do because it "may help someone out who needs to hear a story like yours," as I shared my struggles in life with her (in hopes of encouraging her to fight on). Although I was trying to encourage her to be strong, she was the one actually encouraging me like she had done with so many others. Kaiya was wise beyond her years.

Kaiya, simply put, I love and miss you! A donation will be made to the Cystic Fibrosis Foundation in Kaiya's name.

Now back at the United States Air Force Expedition Center (USAF EC), I would find myself working for the commanding general directly. I would become his Director of Protocol, which entailed taking care of the general and all VIPs that visited the USAF EC. The general had an unlimited supply of energy and he was what you would consider a "general's general." That meant that all customs and courtesies that were supposed to be afforded to him would be, with no exception.

Having been a logistician my entire military career, I had no clue when it came to protocol, although all of the general's supporting staff that I worked with said that I was doing a "good job," so I guess on that note I was doing okay. However, I was not a fan of protocol at all, and it was not the job that I was hired for; but in the military you do the job that is placed before you, and do it well. I put a smile on my face every morning that I walked into the office but truth be told, I hated the job. I was not a tea or coffee and how many sugars type of troop.

As a logistician, I was use to logistics, which entailed people, equipment, and moving assets from one area of responsibility to another. My knuckles dragged the ground and I wanted to perform the duties that I was initially hired for, serving as the Director of the Air Expeditionary Group Staff Course. It was a position that would take deploying senior leaders and give them insight on the missions in Iraq and Afghanistan by way of classified briefings and video teleconferences. Protocol was a far cry from this. Gerri Lynn, who I called the "Oracle" and also worked in the general's office, kept me ahead of the game and out of trouble. I was grateful for her help, and she was my walking "Protocol for Dummies" guide while I tried to keep my head above water in that position, (having never gone to a formal protocol school).

Eventually, a new general would take over command. He was very personable (to include his wife) and although a two-star general, he was by far one of the most humble human beings that I had ever met in my life. His scope of responsibility and range of authority would span the U.S. amongst multiple units. However, he always made time to ask me how the family was doing, and he never let me pass by his office without saying hello while I was working directly for him.

He was a stark contrast from the previous general, yet I personally respected him greatly as an individual (he already had the given respect as a general). He would call on me to work an Armed Services Committee visit to the USAF EC by a Congressman, which let me know that he trusted in me. His selection meant everything to me, and I did everything in my power to ensure that the committee visit was executed with military precision.

He knew I was not a fan of protocol, although I kept a great poker face on. Oddly enough, he called me into his office after being on the job for a few months and said, "Sean, you are doing a good job in protocol, but we are going to get you into the position that we hired you for." It was music to my ears! In time, I moved out of the front office with the general and into my 422 Joint Tactics Squadron (422 JTS) position as a Director. I guess the general said, "thanks for giving it the college try, Sean, but serving coffee and cream is not your cup of tea (pardon the pun)." I guess after all of my years in the military, I still had a hardened exterior about me that did not say "protocol or coffee or cream."

Once I began to work in my final duty position before I officially retired, things settled down for me at the 422 Joint Tactics Squadron. I knew this was my last assignment in the military and I valued each day that I had left in uniform. The troops that were assigned to the squadron made my job that much more enjoyable and I looked forward to taking part in unit functions daily.

However, before I would officially retire from the military, Plainfield, New Jersey would ask me to return as a native son. I was going to be inducted into the Plainfield High School Hall of Fame. It was a tremendous honor, one that said "Sean, we are proud of you!" Plainfield was the birthplace of public education in New Jersey and I had learned so much in Plainfield, not only in the classroom, but also in those inner city streets and life!

I was being inducted for my mentoring and humanitarian efforts around the world. I felt that this was a tremendous honor and I was humbled by the nomination. Reflecting on my struggles as a youth, and especially going through high school, I felt blessed to be considered for induction into the Hall of Fame. Plainfield, NJ is rich in its history—from actors to dancers, professors, artist, doctors, politicians, and lawyers; they all call Plainfield home. Yet, it was a tough town (more so, on the West End). Even Hollywood took note of the mean streets of Plainfield, making reference to it in a *Die Hard* movie stating that the lead character, "Was the 007 of Plainfield, New Jersey;" a place that it was not so easy growing up, thus explaining the toughness of the character depicted in the movie by Bruce Willis.

When I left Plainfield as a young man, I had barely escaped in one piece. To put it bluntly, I was a wreck that by chance found a way to make it out of a given way of life (the streets). Yes, it was a conscious choice to leave, but it was easier said than done. I remembered having to complete two senior years, and the struggles that went along with returning to high school and being a young father. Hope, resiliency and perseverance in life had taken me from the doors of abuse, abandonment, and poverty, to the doors of the Hall of Fame.

I would accept the award on behalf of all of those who had to fight for everything single thing in life. I was not born with a silver spoon in my mouth; I was born of the streets, like any other inner city kid in Chicago, Detroit, Los Angeles, New York, Philadelphia or inner-city America. It shows that you don't have to be an athlete or rapper to make it out of a given situation. I applaud those who make it in those industries, but the reality of it is, the percentages are against you to make it that way as I stated before. Education opened the doors in my life, and education would now walk me into the doors of the Hall of Fame. The American dream is possible for anyone. The percentages are with you and not against you with an education. You just have to believe! Education is afforded to everyone, what you do with it will open the world up to you.

The day of my induction, dignitaries from throughout the state were in attendance as the state proclamations were read. It was a gala affair and my family (brothers, sisters, cousins, aunts, and friends) were all in attendance to celebrate this day, our day. As my son sat out in the audience, I dedicated my speech to him, my only son. Instead of my children seeing their father from behind bars, had I chosen the "other fork in the road" years back, they were instead seeing their father being honored by the place that he called home. When I looked out into the audience I remember thinking to myself, yes, life is remarkable.

I would share a brief conversation with one of the teachers that had a positive influence on me when I was a complete derelict in high school, Mr. S. Marsh.

Mr. Marsh would share a story with me that day that I forgot about. He would remind me of the time that he pulled me to the side in high school and told me that I could go to any school in the country, if I just applied myself. However, during that time in high school, it fell on deaf ears. I thanked him for believing in me back then when I didn't believe in myself, and that he was there to support me now. Moreover, and unbeknownst to me, he had followed my civic and military career over the years. He said something to me the day of my induction ceremony that meant more than any award that I had ever received meant. He said, "Sean, I'm proud of you," words that still resonate with me to this day deeply. He then firmly shook my hand, nodded in approval, gave me a slight pat on the arm, and then took a seat amongst the audience.

When the induction ceremony came to a conclusion, like I had done many years before after my high school graduation, I told my wife of twenty plus years that I would meet up with her and the family in a little while. Like I had done the day of my graduation in 1987, I went up to the very high school that had just inducted me into its Hall of Fame. At the time of my induction, there had been no more than a hundred Alumni that had been inducted into the Plainfield High School Hall of Fame in its century long history, and I was now humbly one of them.

I found myself in the very same place that I had stood the year I graduated. This time, unlike then, I was not just reflecting on what it took for me to graduate, but that life had placed me back there by the grace of God as a humbled man. I thought about Mrs. White-James, my Guidance Counselor back then and the Scared Straight Program and how it literally changed my life, and how I so desperately wanted to thank her. I thought about how many people had written me off and given up on me and the ones who did not. I thought about all my friends that were no longer with us, and how this day was as much theirs as it was mine (street soldiers of the East and the West End and across the nation). I thought again, standing in front of my high school, how anything in life was possible and not . . . impossible. I thought about the Bastard Child and how through it all, somehow I was still standing, "My head bloodied but unbowed." I was no longer ashamed of what I saw in the mirror anymore. With the Plainfield High School Hall of Fame induction behind me, it was now time for me to retire from the United States Air Force.

The planning had begun for my ceremony and I was excited. J. Brooks, a former 353ʳᵈ SOG Special Operations troop, Devil Raider from the 621ˢᵗ Contingency Responses Group and friend, told me about a position that was available in the local school districts where he was now working after retirement. I thanked him for thinking of me for this position as we had a great working relationship while on active duty.

The position was for a Senior Aerospace Instructor. It was the same officer position that Lieutenant Colonel Ruble held when I was first introduced to the Air Force Junior Reserve Officer Training Program at Plainfield High School so many years ago. Life truly had come full circle. Where my life started to change for the better decades back in the JROTC program (my roots), I would now find myself there again, this time as the senior officer. Never in a million years could I have envisioned this, me, a JROTC Instructor. Lieutenant Colonel Ruble saw so much more in me than I did in myself back then.

After interviewing with the school district and being hired for the position, it was time to "hang up the uniform" as we say on active duty. But, before I separated, the United States Air Force Expeditionary Center Commander would have me accompany him on one final military temporary duty assignment before saying goodbye to the Air Force. It was his way of saying, "Sean, thank you for a long and fruitful career." He would also serve as my presiding official for my formal retirement.

To my surprise, the general had selected me to go to the New York Stock Exchange (NYSE) to ring the closing bell that signified the end of trading for the day. The NYSE had rolled out the "Red Carpet" for us. From the trader floor, to the inner chambers of the exchange, nothing was off limits for us. We were each given a medallion, which was personally inscribed for our visit. We got to mix and mingle with the NYSE "brass" and they were very inviting. We even got to touch gifts from around the world that literally costs millions of dollars that were sent to the Exchange. I got to stand at the podium with the Exchange gavel as I looked out over the Board Room floor. No expense was spared for our visit.

When the moment came to close the New York Stock Exchange, the general had me stand right beside him and his wife. He looked at me and said, "Sean get up here, this is your moment as much as it is mine!" The humility of this man was incredible. In that moment, in front of the world, with millions of people watching from around the globe, his concern was not of them, but of me, and saying thank you for your military service to our nation. I am eternally grateful for that humbling gesture on the general's behalf!

Remember this about life. Regardless of the start, no matter how dire, believe in yourself and the power of education. I had come from the war torn streets of Central New Jersey, during the height of the crack invasion, (the belly of the beast) to the Board Room of the New York Stock Exchange, the epicenter of the financial world.

Sadly, right before my retirement ceremony, I would lose a very good friend and comrade in arms to a suicide bomber in Afghanistan. In all of my years in the military, through the many missions, I had never lost anyone so close to me in uniform. I could not wrap my mind around it all. We were flight commanders together in the 816th Contingency Response Group. When I heard about his death, I was hurt beyond words. It was surreal to hear that he had been Killed in Action. Major D. Gray was one of the best officers that I had ever known. He was a "man's man," and you could not find a soul that would have anything negative to say about him. Now retiring, it was a stark reminder of the cost of freedom, and Major Gray willingly stepped up to the challenge and gave his life in defense of our great nation. I would dedicate my military retirement ceremony to him in his honor. Additionally, I would also name the Kitty Hawk Air Society (the Air Force Honor Society for JROTC) after him in his memory at my new school as the Senior Aerospace Instructor. A portion of the proceeds of this book will be donated to the Wounded Warrior Project in his honor.

The day of my retirement had finally arrived; it was a beautiful and perfect day. It was a packed house with every seat filled; some even standing in the aisles. Entering the auditorium, I looked around to see the many faces that were in attendance for the ceremony. Many of my childhood friends had come out to support me on this important day. William Wray, my right-hand man, Renee Sterling, who stood by my side during my Special Operation days and as a friend over the years, Keith Bilal, who was the voice of reason years back when I was caught up in the hustle, and Randy McKinney, yes, my childhood friend and brother figure, was there to share in this momentous day.

When the general and I took our seats on the stage, I looked out into the sea of people and I fought back my emotions; each of them there to say *Sean, well done, we are proud of you.* I was humbled by the moment. As the general began to give his remarks recapping my service to the nation, I remember looking at my family in the front row, my wife and children, my sister, brothers, my father, and My Aunt Cynthia. It had taken a lifetime to get to this point, and it was a moment that I was proud to share with each person in the room, but most important, my family. My time had finally come to say goodbye to the institution that had afforded my family and me so much.

I reflected on my struggles from when I first joined the Air Force. I thought about the opportunities that the Air Force had provided. I thought about the travels and the people that I had met the world over. I thought about the highs and the lows of life, and that some had even suggested that I was, "Better off dead" when I was just a youth just trying to survive in the streets of Central New Jersey. But as I sat there, I knew I had done one simple thing in life—I made a change for the better. I also knew that I had made a positive difference in the lives of others. Sitting there, I asked myself *what would I have done in life had I not joined the military, or taken the other fork in the road? Would I even still be alive?* I had lost so many of my friends by this point to street violence and jail. Again sitting there I asked myself, *would I be in jail?* God had truly watched over the Bastard Child, and for that, I was eternally grateful.

At the conclusion of the general's speech, I presented each of my children with the "Children's Medal," for understanding the needs of the Air Force mission and never complaining when I had to leave the family for an extended period of time. My children would always greet me with open arms at the door upon my return from the many deployments, a small gesture that meant everything in the world to me. Tonya, my wife of 20 plus years, the one that said, "Sean you have to go back to school" so many years before and the mother of my children, I thanked for being a supportive and understanding military spouse, a daunting and difficult task. Yes, that 12-year-old girl that I had met so many years ago in the corner store of Plainfield that said "Sean I'm going to marry you one day" was indeed a prophet, still faithfully by my side some 30 years later.

I thanked my father, who would turn out to be one of my biggest heroes and supporters in life. As I became a man, I realized that the battles between my father and my mother were grounded in my father wanting to simply raise his son, not just me, but also all of his children. I would honor him in front of everyone that day. Good, bad, or indifferent, my father tried to keep all of his children under one roof as long as he could. Sadly, my mother was no longer a part of my life. The pain and scars from years past had finally taken divisive roots in our relationship. I was no longer a naïve child but a forgiving man. Inside I had made peace with mother, who I love still to this day, despite all that I had been through as a child and teenager by her hand.

Before the ceremony would conclude, the general would present me with the Presidential Volunteer Service medal for my public service, a medal that I will forever cherish as it represents the human spirit, community involvement, and the kindness of man for one that wears the uniform.

With the retirement ceremony drawing to a close, it was time for the two things that a military person knows are coming regarding their retirement. It is where most people get "choked up and watery eyed" before saying goodbye to the uniform. The military Shadow Box is a going away gift that is presented to the member that is separating from the service. It is an incased glass gift that has all of your awarded military honors inside of it. In part, it is a summary of your military career. The general would present me my shadow box, and it was beautiful. Looking at it, it put my military career in context for me, I was thankful for the hand of God who had protected me over the many years of service and that I was there to receive it in front of those who meant everything to me, as they supported me over the many years in the military.

The final item that I was to receive the day of my retirement was the United States flag. It had been flown over Joint Base McGuire-Dix-Lakehurst in New Jersey by a C-17 aircraft in honor of my retirement. All members of the military know that this is the final gesture of a nation and the military saying farewell to you and thank you for your service as it is presented to you.

The Master of Ceremony for my retirement asked me to please come forward as the nation's colors would now be presented to me in honor of my service to the country. Although a short distance, each step that I took towards the center of the stage seemed like a mile. It was time to say goodbye to the institution that I had grown to love, where I had become a patriot, where I would understand what love of country meant, and where I would gladly do it all over, even give my life if called upon again.

The two Non-Commissioned Officers slowly made their way down the aisle carrying my retirement flag; they were methodical, professional, and each step they took towards center stage, towards me, represented the end of my military career. I had seen many retirements over the years, the very ceremony that I was now taking part in, and I always wondered why the member became so emotional; I quickly understood why (love of country). I fought back my emotions as I stood center stage.

The flag was unfolded and the Stars and Stripes were displayed to all in attendance, I stood there motionless but with a ton of emotions, I fought to hold my military bearing. When the two Non-Commissioned Officers began to in-case the flag again, I could see my son who had been placed in the center seat opposite of me. The lights were drawn in on me and the presenter of the colors, the rest of the auditorium was dark. No one dared whisper a word as the flag transitioned from his hands to my arms, (right over left held tightly to my body). He honored the flag with a "slow-hand-salute" and then did an about-face, as the other Non-Commissioned Officer fell in and they marched off into the darkened room.

I slowly marched over to my son, my legacy, with a slight facing movement. With the eyes of the world now focused on a father and son, (those who meant everything to me that were in attendance) I approached him. As he rose to his feet, I presented my most coveted military keepsake to him, the one that I had just received (my retirement flag).

It was an emotional moment as the tears began to stream down from my eyes, as well as his. My son understood in that moment that I was proudly passing my legacy on to him; his raising out of his seat was a symbolic gesture that he was ready to rise up and accept that responsibility of manhood, to answer a nation's call if called upon one day. Once my son had our nation's colors firmly in his possession, I saluted the flag with a slow-hand-salute, returning it to my side slowly. I returned to center stage knowing that my son could now carry a hard-earned legacy forward.

I knew that day that a son was proud of his father and it meant everything, the world to me! The Bastard Child did not end up dead or in jail, as many in my youth had prophesized. I had humbly risen from the streets of New Jersey to become a non-commissioned officer, an officer, a family man, a humanitarian, a friend, a mentor, an educator and someone that my wife, children, friends and family could all be proud of in the end. I offer up my life story and all of the events that surround it, to inspire the fingers that turn the pages of this book that thinks life's impossible. Again I say, believe in yourself! Like everything God created, my life has a purpose—to share my life story with the world, to serve as his living testament of perseverance. You too have a purpose . . .

In closing, Sean in the book of names means, "A gift from God." This book is what I would like to give to the world through God's grace and the sparing of my life in 2008. It is written for all, but it is dedicated to those who think they have little to no chance in this world, who share in my struggles and feel that they have been kicked and beaten by this thing we call life and asks, "why me?" Remember what I stated in the beginning of the book, "No one said that life would be easy." Ultimately, I knew deep inside that I was a good man that wanted to do right by all mankind. I knew that I needed to make a change in my life; education would be that key!

I owed it to every American that has ever worn the uniform and shed blood for our freedom, who made the ultimate sacrifice, so that one day I, and others, would have an opportunity at the American Dream, to try. I owed it to the Buffalo Soldiers and the Tuskegee Airmen who came before me and paved the way, to try. I owed it to those across the fabric of America who made the sacrifices throughout our nation's storied history of all races; most important I owed it to myself to try.

I stated in the beginning that I am no pro athlete; I am but one man with a simple story of hope to share—a story that many others across our great nation share, but their voices go unheard. I come from very humble beginnings, yet I am someone, to somebody. I am grateful for the extraordinary life that God has bestowed upon me to live, even as the Bastard Child. Although beaten, abused, homeless, and not given much in the way of life, I am grateful for . . . my life!

Yes, I still wakeup in a bed full of sweat at times from events past, plagued forever by the physical and deep-rooted mental abuse of my youth; but as the great poet Maya Angelo once stated, "But still, I rise." Believe in yourself; results, not excuses, will change your circumstances. Remember, the percentages are in your favor with an education, than without an education, and the power to change your life is in your hands. Thank you to everyone who believed in me and helped me along in my journey; I am eternally grateful. I would also like to thank Author Dawn L. Forte' for her help with this project . . . I am forever in your debt Dawn! Remember, this is not the end of my story, but only the beginning of it . . .

Before the completion of my autobiography, my brother Kirk would tragically lose his life. His last words to me on the day of my military retirement (the last time we would ever speak to one another) were, "You did things the way they should be done and I'm proud of you; I'm glad you're home for good now, I love you."

I love you too Kirk; you will be missed dearly little brother. May you rest in peace. A portion of the proceeds from this book will be donated to a Plainfield, New Jersey Stop the Violence Program in his memory.

I have poured my soul into every page of this book, and if it changes just one life for the better, then it has served its purpose. Remember, "Judge me not by the heights I have reached, but by the depth from which I have come."

—Frederick Douglass

—The Bastard Child . . .

"Ganbatte"

Made in the USA
Middletown, DE
24 January 2020